Once Upon a Time
on a Bicycle

by Michael Russell

This work depicts events in
the life of the author. Some dialogue has
been paraphrased and/or combined;
some names have been changed.

ONCE UPON A TIME ON A BICYCLE
Copyright © 2018, 2023 by Michael Russell

ALL RIGHTS RESERVED

Excepting brief quotations in critical
articles or reviews, no part of this work
may be used or reproduced in any manner
whatsoever without written permission from the
publisher. For correspondence and inquiries, or to
order multiple copies of this book, please visit:

nonesmanneslond.com

Nonesmanneslond
32.7089649°N, -108.5381073°W

Russell, Michael, 1957 -
Once Upon a Time on a Bicycle

ISBN 978-0-9998730-0-7
Trade Paperback

Once Upon a Time on a Bicycle is available in hardcover
and trade-paperback bindings. Editions Nonesmanneslond
publishes ink-on-paper books exclusively.

SECOND EDITION

2018

For Alonso Quijano, Cyrano de Bergerac,
Arthur Winslow, Howard Roark, Shane,
Sam Flint, and Lucas McCain –
with gratitude to the writers
who gave them life.

2023

Near Teakettle just north of the highway, the Belize River, the Old River, meandered to the Atlantic from its origin out of the Macal and Mopan near San Ignacio. To the south Renati could see, like feathery pencil shadings slanted over the emerald edge of the distant Mayan Mountains, rain. Ahead, beyond an ever-nearing everchanging panorama, he studied a vision less tangible: clear at its center, undefined at its borders, indefinite in its distance.

For that vision, still clear,
now defined and definite.
Made real.

"I do not insist," answered Don Quixote,
"that this is a full adventure,
but it is the beginning of one,
for this is the way adventures begin."

The Ingenious Gentleman Don Quixote of La Mancha
Miguel de Cervantes Saavedra, 1605

Contents

Preface   ix

Prologue   3

Stage One: Seeking Tabula Rasa   5

Stage Two: Stranger in a Strange Land   85

Stage Three: The Road to La Mancha   199

Epilogue   267

Notes From the Road   271

Preface

When I decided to ride, only *the ride* mattered. I was not inclined to take photographs or keep a journal, push for hundred-mile days or bemoan twenty, climb such-and-such a pass or employ so-and-so's equipment or be the first whoever to do whatever. But since I could permit myself no unfulfilled responsibilities, it took almost two years to finally be riding. During that seemingly endless preparatory period, while contemplating my journey as a "once upon a time" endeavor and after dubbing my bicycle in honor of my thirty-year relationship with Miguel de Cervantes Saavedra's masterwork, I discovered that I wanted to keep a record.

But not as a travelogue or how-to guide.

My manner of coming at life has manifestly been shaped by characters in fiction whose qualities I admire. Virtuous acts proceeding from just principles have inspired me since I was a child, although I could probably not have articulated *why* until I was in my late teens. Correspondingly, I have long considered the obligatory grownup-to-young-person question, "What do you want to be when you grow up?" as essentially meaningless except as a postscript to:

"*Who* do you want to be?"

I was four months from starting my ride, gazing through a train window across the predawn plains of North Dakota while listening to an audio rendition of Richard Wheeler's *Flint's Gift*, when I grasped that what I wanted was to someday re-experience my journey the same way I was experiencing Sam Flint's. I resolved then and there to pen *Once Upon a Time on a Bicycle* in the third person, and, for the *línea de demarcación* I believed my ride would represent, I traded my fifty-six-year-old surname for a new one.

About a million pedal revolutions later, over afternoon coffee at a restaurant in Poptún, El Petén, a Guatemalan gentleman referred to me, no doubt complimentarily, as an adventurer. "No, I'm not," I countered with surprising defensiveness. When he replied, "But you are having some big adventure, no?" I politely conceded his observation and, while riding the next day, pondered the motive for my mildly indignant response.

If an adventurer is, as Merriam-Webster defines the term, "someone who seeks dangerous or exciting experiences," I am not such a person. I am, rather, someone who, having chosen a path according to a standard not governed by fear, may find himself in dangerous or exciting experiences. Life seen through independent eyes and pursued as an irreplaceable value will seldom be safe or dull, no matter what one's vocation or non-thrill-seeking hobbies.

In the course of transcribing *Once Upon a Time on a Bicycle* from handwritten journals, voice notes recorded while astride a leather saddle, and memory, I have found myself time and again validating what Michael Renati realized while squinting into the late-morning sun a few miles east of San Antonio.

I was right to ride.

Michael Russell
February 2018

Once Upon a Time on a Bicycle

(a self-propelled two-wheeled journey of necessity)

Prologue

Through the window of my cabin I see his motionless form beneath a blanket in the snow. It helps knowing he lived the best dog's life ever: bounding with the enchanting joy of a puppy through an endless Rocky Mountain forest; surveying a domain where elk, deer, and moose routinely graced the vista; treeing a black bear and wondering what next to do; learning after his third encounter the defining characteristic of porcupines; sleepily supervising his best pal's solo construction of a wilderness homestead. It helps knowing he knew at the end that I loved him and would never leave him, but for twelve years he was my shadow and now he is not.

I miss my shadow, my Ragnar.

I will bury him today in the frozen ground of a sunny forest glade, find for my secluded mountain property a worthy owner, and help to establish in her new life the incomparable friend who kept me upright through an undoing I had never imagined possible. With my belongings reduced to what I can carry on my bicycle, accompanied by what I have so far learned and achieved, I will begin peddling south.

Ushuaia sounds about right.

I have been a business manager, logger, photographer, writer, waiter, theater actor, dishwasher, landscaper, builder, mechanic, musician, teacher, bartender, and professional athlete. When next I compose in the pages of this journal I will be a nomad.

STAGE ONE

Seeking Tabula Rasa

Often when I have camped here,
it has made me want to become the ground,
become the water, become the trees, mix with
the whole thing. Not know myself from it.
Never unmix again. Why is that?

The Virginian: A Horseman of the Plains
Owen Wister, 1902

One

Michael Renati signed his name to the last of the thirteen letters he had written at a picnic table in a sun-soaked park on the southern reach of San Diego Bay. He addressed the thirteenth envelope and folded the single page into it, but stopped short of sealing away what he had written. He felt a panic in his pulse and a familiar trepidation in his breathing: forty months had come and gone and, still, even the most tenuous reminder could empty him like a blade through a vein. He removed his reading glasses and placed them upside down over a corner of the envelope.

Maybe he would mail it tomorrow, or after he had been riding for a while. It was, after all, the final item on his list and he still had a few more tasks to complete.

Two days earlier he had sold to a young man from El Cajon the 1991 Mitsubishi Montero that carried him and his bicycling gear from Montana to California by way of Arizona. Tonight he would leave the remainder of his past-life clothing – including the shirt, jeans, and sneakers he now wore – in a disabled-veterans donation box inside the entrance to Denny's on E Street. It was . . . *something* . . . he thought, unable to find a better word, to own by choice less than his body weight in personal property.

Thirty-five pounds less, he calculated, counting the edibles in his pantry bag and almost seven quarts of water. He had reduced his wardrobe, not that he ever needed a walk-in closet, to four combinations: two for on the bicycle, two for off. His sixteen-by-twenty-four board-and-batten workshop now zipped handily into an eight-by-twelve nylon case. His updated kitchen – a cup, a plate, and a bowl; a knife, a fork, and a spoon; a pot, a pan, and a coffee press; a wood-burning stove, a collapsible fabric sink, and a

P38 can opener – was almost poetic, reminding him of the Max Rich prospector ballad performed by Lorne Green. More than once he had imagined some future traveler in the Atacama Desert spying the exposed rim of his sand-drift-buried titanium cup. The thought always made him smile.

His once-extensive library of books, music, and movies – with the exception of a novel in his handlebar bag and a box of handlebar-bag-size volumes ready to mail from Arizona – had been rigorously thinned and installed into a diminutive laptop computer and a triplet of MP3 players. He would sooner dine on acorns and dandelion greens than set forth without the inspiration of good stories and music.

He chose a stamp from the few that remained in his book of twenty and pressed it onto the thirteenth envelope. He slid his glasses into their case. *There's no point in reading this again*, he thought as he removed and unfolded and read the letter again.

On the walk back to his hotel he transferred twelve missives from his laptop bag into a street-corner mailbox. The moment the blue steel door clanged shut the word that had eluded him earlier came to mind. It was not "something" to own almost nothing, he realized. It was *good*. He reopened the mailbox door and held it down with his left elbow, extracted the thirteenth envelope from his bag, and tossed it in.

HE MADE CAMP THE FOLLOWING EVENING under a broad live-oak canopy twenty-two miles east of Chula Vista, fifty feet from a thicket-shrouded deep stream. The direction of the water's flow reminded him that tomorrow would be a day of climbing, and he could hear from his tent – when the whine of rubber on pavement relented – the current's gentle chortling. The songbirds that joined him just before sundown seemed oblivious to the disturbance. Traffic noise, he granted with reluctance, was inescapably along for the ride.

He washed in the stream and prepared a cold supper with hot tea. The air chilled soon after dark; he bundled into his sleeping bag and reviewed his day.

The partial knee-ligament tear he had sustained three years earlier and reinjured while clearing a fallen Douglas fir from his – no, he reminded himself, from *Roy's* – primitive driveway during a September snowstorm bothered him less than he had anticipated. The theories he had employed when designing his expedition bicycle, his Rocinante, had been verified as worthy, although he suspected it would take a few more dismounts before he stopped reaching down to loosen toe-clip straps.

His ponderous slow-motion tip-over at a red light on Hilltop Drive would probably help him remember.

This was not his country and the evening sounds were strange, but the familiar shriek of coyotes in the black of early morning brought his body upright and his mind to where he had heard them last. For two years he had rehearsed saying goodbye to that wild mountain meadow and to the cabin that had been home while he built *home*. Why was it so hard to believe he had done so for real? He settled again onto his air mattress, hoping he would not dream of what every drawknife-peeled, scribe-fit pine log represented.

But he did dream of it.

He awakened without opening his eyes, discerning through his lids and the ecru nylon of his tent that dawn was near. The brook, as if emboldened after a sequestering winter night, murmured mellifluously, tunefully. From the unstructured chords he gleaned piano, steel guitar, a breathy baritone ...

Four walls to hear me, four walls to see,
Four walls too near me, closing in on me.

As a child he spent many an evening in his father's three-position Naugahyde recliner, listening in the dark to songs from his parents' LP-record collection: Jim Reeves, Johnny Mathis, Nat King Cole, Al Martino. When he discovered music outside his home it was soulful ballads that brought from within him the kind of energy and strength his peers found in popular rock tunes. "My Heroes Have Always Been Cowboys" had propelled him over yesterday's toughest grade.

He wondered why he found power in the sad songs.

A HUNDRED MILES FROM THE PACIFIC, the Yuha Desert opened before him with long flats and beckoning straight lines. He had taken the three thousand-foot Interstate descent into Ocotillo in two stages, breaking for thirty minutes among colossal boulders above a wash to read a chapter of T. Jefferson Parker's *Silent Joe* as his rims cooled. It had been three years since he had read that novel while riding along the coast of the Sea of Cortez. The page that contained the line, "It's a terrible emptiness to feel your own history dissolve," was still marked by a tooth-edged blade of grass, now brown.

He felt undeservedly guilty about starting his ride with two short days, even though he had resolved to have no distance expectations. California 94 through the mountains between Otay Lakes Road and Campo had been stamina-sapping. Whether sitting in a low gear or standing on a taller one, he felt every pound of the hundred and thirty-five underneath him. His recurring question, "When will one of these speeding motorcyclists lose it on a curve?" was answered a few miles above Barrett Junction when a machinery-rending percussion three hundred yards ahead was followed by horrific screaming and a rising plume of white smoke. He had stopped the lead rider and suggested he return to check on his comrade. By then it was dusk and his quadriceps felt like wood, so he rested for a few minutes before walking Rocinante another hundred yards uphill and making a tent-less camp on sloping rocky ground to the unsettling clamor of gathering emergency vehicles.

He had slept hard, but low-flying border-patrol helicopters startled him twice in the dark and a hummingbird buzzed him awake at dawn. After breakfasting on dried fruit and granola he had climbed higher into the sunrise and a headwind, and stopped ninety minutes later for coffee at a roadside cafe.

Now, pushing hard to make up for time he knew he hadn't lost, realizing he would have to reconcile some habituated remnant of self-competitiveness, he enjoyed both the achievement and the relief of having his first days, more demanding than expected, behind him. And, he thought with further contentment, seventy-two degrees on a sunny afternoon in the middle of winter felt wonderful.

RIDING INTO CALEXICO two hours after sundown over bone-jarring broken pavement felt less so. He checked into the first budget motel he passed and was asleep ten minutes after stepping out of a twenty-minute shower. He rose in the morning to find Rocinante listing glumly over flat tires.

Two

In a grocery-store parking lot east of Yuma a portly young man herding shopping carts asked Renati where he was from, then where he was bound.

"On a bike?" the fellow asked doubtfully.

"*Bicycle*," Renati corrected. He slapped Rocinante's saddle with the flat of his hand. "On *this* bicycle."

The young man's face went blank. "Why?" he asked.

At the top of Telegraph Pass seven miles later Renati answered, "Because a truly good bicycle is a perfect integration of human anatomy and mechanical engineering."

Rocinante corroborated with a soft upshift click, then a second and a third, as he and Renati accelerated together into a restorative descent.

A GENERATION OF BICYCLE TECHNOLOGY had come and gone without Renati's notice. He had allowed his cycling-publication subscriptions to lapse, and he had not leafed through a parts catalog since building up a tandem frame in 1989 for an injury-foreshortened ride from New Hampshire to Arizona. But he had spent most of those years honing skills as a designer, builder, and problem solver, and his function-premised theories seldom failed in practice. He distrusted fashion and trends on principle, and although he would never reject a product because it was popular, popularity made him skeptical. He couldn't help but feel annoyance with innovations that separated users from their relationship to, and consequently their understanding of, a device and its function.

"Same great product, exciting new look!" usually prompted

him to buy another brand.

He had no idea which manufacturers were still in business or who was making what, but the moment he saw Gary Turner's triple-triangle concept in the form of a used commuter leaning against a weathered wooden fence, he knew he was seeing the frame he would design and build if such was his inclination. He purchased the bicycle and rode it seven hundred miles and parted out the components and shipped the frame to a company in Oregon for powder coating. Then he selected, over the course of a year, the equipment he needed for what he needed it to do. Many of his preferred parts and accessories were a challenge to locate: his forty-hole tandem rims, classic short-pull brake levers, and cleated leather touring shoes were "new old stock;" his handlebar and double-bottle cage were prototypes; his carrier racks were available only from England. He chose racks and panniers conjointly, wondering why manufacturers did not harmoniously integrate both, and spent a month of late winter evenings packing, weighing, and balancing his bags to music that one night chanced to include – and from that night forward always included – Ennio Morricone's soundtrack to *Once Upon a Time in the West*.

He found that the best of the large handlebar bags were manufactured to sit too high, so he trimmed the drops off of a second handlebar and affixed it to a second, shorter stem underneath – gaining five inches of clearance for the aerobars he thought a good idea for headwinds and monotonous flats. The arrangement doubled as a mount for his cyclometer, served as a sealed document holder, and brought the weight of his at-hand accessories – camera, binoculars, telephone, music, wallet, journal, jackknife, paperback book, compass, and flashlight – lower over the steering axis. He designed and built a hinged rear-rack compartment to carry eighteen-inch-long tent poles and to expedite the removal and reinstallation of packed panniers, and fitted an aluminum sleeve containing emergency resources into his seat tube.

Over the course of a year his ideal frame looked more and more like his ideal expedition bicycle. By the time he was lacing spokes, the machine felt like an extension of his mind; he knew it would soon feel like an extension of his body.

A SOUND NIGHT'S SLEEP at the Dateland campground was impossible. The railroad tracks he had been paralleling for the past eighty miles were only a hundred yards from his tent, and at least one train an hour passed at high speed. He dressed and broke camp lackadaisically, and topped off his granola-and-banana breakfast with a date shake at the travel center by the Interstate.

He was tired and grateful for the tailwind, which seemed to be increasing as the day warmed. He listened for a while to an audiobook, but it only made him sleepy. He practiced an exercise he called "seeing the road": composing a mental picture of the terrain ahead, then looking away or closing his eyes while staying on course. He had ridden only a few miles since stopping to make a peanut-butter-and-honey sandwich when he angled down the Sentinel exit and turned left beneath the overpass then right and left again into the gravel parking lot of a lonely desert store. He leaned his bicycle against a stucco wall, withdrew his wallet from his handlebar bag, and walked inside to the reach-in cooler at the back wall. He brought his selection to an elderly Hispanic woman who had not been at the counter when he entered, but who now sat primly on a stool behind it.

She studied the bottle he handed her and told him the price, then paused for a moment to study *him*, her hand suspended above the keys of an old cash register.

"You look familiar," she said.

"Three years ago," he replied.

"The man on the bicycle. The man who built a house in the mountains."

"Yes, ma'am." He tapped the cap of the bottle he had placed on the counter. "I bought the same drink last time."

"We talked for a while."

"You asked why I was riding alone in the desert. Then you asked me to pull up that chair." He pointed to where it still stood to the left of the door.

"Did you go back to . . . to . . ."

"Montana. Yes, I went back."

"Did you find the answers to your questions?"

"Some."

"Did you find God?"

"I spent considerable effort looking for God many years ago."

"And . . . ?" She placed her hand over the open bible on the little table beside her chair.

"I was eighteen, working in northern Michigan. I was one sentence into a prayer for help when I realized I hadn't ever seriously considered the existence of God. I felt foolish and I quit my prayer. Then I read the Christian bible, the Lost Books of the Bible, the Book of Mormon, and parts of the Koran."

"And . . . ?"

"And nothing I read, nothing in my research, nothing in my many conversations with religious people convinced me it could ever be right to explain the natural world by reference to a supernatural one. It felt lazy, arbitrary, like a betrayal."

"I was a Catholic until a few years ago," she said. "Now I'm just a Christian."

"What happened?" he asked.

She described the day she grasped the hypocrisy of weekly confession, then told him it had always troubled her that Catholics had done many bad things in the name of their faith. She told him she hoped he would find what he wanted. He told her he remembered she wanted to sell the store and relocate to California, and that he hoped she would soon find a buyer.

"That's up to God," she said.

He downed his vegetable juice and mounted his bicycle. The speed-limit sign at the top of the onramp read seventy-five. He checked his cyclometer – twenty point four miles per hour – and counted fifteen pedal rotations in ten seconds.

Like the sign says, he thought.

With his forearms cradled in his aerobar rests he hitchhiked a steady tailwind to the passionate chords of Richard Strauss' *Opus 35, Fantastic Variations on a Theme of Knightly Character*.

IT WAS A COOL NIGHT, and he was thankful for it. He had been able to get his gear far enough off the Interstate to enjoy separation from road noise, and he made camp at sunset in the shadow of an ancient bird-pecked saguaro surrounded by thorny scrub. He heated water for washing and coffee, wishing as he pulled on long underwear and a sweater that he had the makings for hot chocolate. He continued fueling his miniature wood stove from a pile of miniature logs – more for the romance of the fire than for warmth – while finishing *Silent Joe* by headlamp.

The sky was moonless, but by eight o'clock the stars shone bright enough for him to walk without a flashlight. He stopped at the top of a low rocky incline and watched cars and trucks passing anonymously four hundred yards to the north on the highway. He assumed the glow in the east to be Phoenix, which twenty-four years ago had been home for four years.

A robust breeze pressed against his back and through his sweater and shirt. He walked downhill from it and sat on the stone-strewn ground, still slightly warmer than the air. Something about the highway traffic made the place feel extra lonely. He liked it. He stayed there, unaware of the passing time or falling temperature, watching the traffic and the glow of the city until he realized he was shivering.

Three

From Casa Grande he paralleled Interstate 10 through Picacho to Tucson, where he followed River Road east and south, looking for evidence of its namesake. Although he occasionally spied a sandy channel with potential, no river was to be found. His knee pained him only slightly, but by the time he reached the top of South Houghton he was unable to flex it past ninety degrees.

He stopped at a convenience store, bought a cup of coffee, and telephoned ahead to extend his campground reservation. He sat beside Rocinante with his back against a painted steel post, sipping his coffee and massaging his knee. He watched a man of about thirty walk hand in hand with a girl of about ten from their car to the store. She wore sparkly pink sneakers and a pink sweatshirt and she smiled at him and waved as they passed. The question that crossed his mind the instant he returned her greeting was one he never could have imagined only last summer, and he hated that it was now part of his consciousness. The man smiled at him, too, from under the brim of a baseball cap.

He turned and pinched Rocinante's rear tire. It was slightly soft, as he had come to expect. Between thorns and retread wire he was averaging one flat every – he did the division – seventy miles.

HE HAD KNOWN THE GIRL since she was seven. He knew her older brother and younger sister. He thought he knew her parents. By the time she was nine she had befriended him in a way that suggested an unusual level of trust or need. He attended her small-town music-class recitals and escorted her and her mother and grandmother to their first professional symphony concert. The girl was enchanted. He bought her a subscription to a classical-music magazine and, with her parents' permission, gave her a Christmas gift of private lessons with a teacher who taught professionals. The girl was invited by the teacher to study daily after school; within a year, music had become her world.

But two months into her second year she tearfully told Renati that her parents were trying to get her to quit, telling her she was wasting her time and that they missed who she "used to be," and that they were saying "awful things" about him. One day, the girl's mother removed her bodily from class. A few weeks later the music teacher received a square of folded paper, passed along in secret by one of the girl's friends. It read:

> I don't know what to do now. I'll keep fighting and I won't give up. But this isn't only music, this is everything. This is my career, my passion, my best friend, everyone I love, everyone who truly loves me. I'm so scared. And I need help. I'm having difficulty handling all this alone and I don't know if I can. If there is any way, please help me. Please.

The teacher gave the note to Child Protective Services, and soon after received another.

> My parents say somebody called and they might be investigated for abuse. I don't know who called, when the investigation will take place and what will happen. But I think this investigation needs to happen as soon as possible. My parents have a friend who is a card reader that my mom talks to nearly every day to be ahead of anything anyone is doing to help me. Also my parents are telling many relatives and friends about everything that is happening. Except, of course, they're leaving out the whole truth. And twisting everything so that Michael, you, and me are awful people. I don't know what this investigation really is? I'm not physically

abused. So there isn't really any physical evidence. All I have to show is truth and honesty. My parents seem to think that if this investigation happens I'll get taken away from here. But, if I go, where will I go? Has anyone considered that? Do I get thrown into a place for abused children? Do I get put up for adoption?

Neither the teacher nor Renati was apprised of the results of an investigation, but eventually they heard that the mother had moved east with the children while the father stayed behind.

Three and a half years passed. Renati was six months from starting his ride, driving a loop through Virginia, Tennessee, and Arkansas visiting friends he hadn't seen in decades. He was in Gatlinburg when he received a message from the girl through a photo-sharing website. She was attending an advanced summer music camp, still dreaming of becoming a professional, hoping that the hosting school would ask her to stay. His next scheduled stop was to visit a pianist-composer with whom he had worked in musical theater, now a professor at a university two miles from where the girl was enrolled.

He met her in a public park. They toured a nearby museum, then spent the afternoon walking together outdoors, sharing news. She had recently turned sixteen, and although he recognized the girl he had known years ago, she displayed a self-conscious disquietude unfamiliar to him. Perhaps it had always been there, he thought, to a lesser degree. He was, he knew, slow to notice such things.

She said her mother told people they moved to be close to her maternal grandfather. She said she thought her brother used drugs and was in a gang and that Renati probably wouldn't know him, and that she was worried about her little sister going "home" for a week to visit their father, but she declined to say why. He told her about his long-ago life in Tennessee and Arkansas, and about his upcoming bicycle expedition. While riding in his rental car back to her accommodations she asked, "May I say a bad word?"

He had laughed and replied, "Of course."

After a long moment of silence she whispered, "My father's a bastard."

She seemed to shrink into the passenger seat, hugging herself as if chilled. She turned away and stared out the window. He passed her street and drove for another minute, then turned into a golf-course parking lot, stopped, and switched off the engine.

"Would you like to walk some more?" he asked.

On a bridge over a boggy streamed bisecting the north nine holes, through uncontrollable tears and sudden fits of violent convulsions, the girl told him why her father was a bastard. In a moment of horror he realized that she had been trying to tell him for years.

"Remember a long time ago when we were helping you decorate for Christmas and I said I liked being seven better than eight?" she asked.

"Yes," he replied, "but that was all you would say."

"When I turned eight he told me it was time to do what big girls do."

She wept for twenty minutes in his arms, remembering bits and pieces aloud, standing on the bridge in growing darkness. He held her hand as they walked back to the parking lot. Outside the car she asked in a quivering voice, "Is there anything I could have done to make him . . . you know?"

He tried to assure her that it was impossible for her to have brought such a thing on herself, but she was sobbing again and seemed not to be listening. "Do you think my mother knew?" she interrupted suddenly, her question a stricken gasp.

Of course not, he wanted to reply, but their house had been tiny, a single crowded level overflowing with the stuff of working parents and young children. He recalled the room she shared with her brother: their bunk bed, her stuffed-animal collection, a door to a short hallway leading to the parents' room. There was scarcely enough space in the house for a private conversation, and in her outpouring she had said: *He would take me to their room. My mother wasn't there. I think she was in the room behind the kitchen.*

He had never seen the room behind the kitchen, but heard it was a space at the rear of the house they were "working on." He hugged her again, searching for the right words.

"I'm so sorry," was the best he could do.

He sent her a prepaid cell phone for the day when she would need a lifeline and made arrangements with his bank to open a savings account for when she turned eighteen. He read as much as he could stomach about incest and child sexual abuse.

"One in four," a magazine article claimed. Had he ever pondered such a question he might have guessed one in a million.

Her first call for help came four months later while he was staying with friends in Arizona, preparing for his ride. Her brother, recently returned to live with their father, had told her that morning in a text message that he was going to commit suicide.

"What should I do?" she asked in a panic.

The second call came on the heels of the first, to her former music teacher. Her mother, the girl explained, was sending her and her sister to spend Christmas with the father.

"I'm ready to report him," she said. "Who do I call?"

As the date of her trip drew near, and after a Child Protective Services employee negligently telephoned the mother, the girl became increasingly worried that her parents suspected her decision and that there would be no one at the airport to protect her.

Renati promised she would be safe when she got off the plane. When she asked if he would be at the airport he told her he would. When she asked "Will I see you?" he told her she would not.

The scene at the terminal unfolded as if rehearsed: the father was intercepted by law-enforcement personnel and the sisters were ushered into a waiting car. They passed within a few feet of Renati at the exit, the older girl's head held high while departing into the night for whatever new world awaited her, the younger girl in tears. Neither noticed a backpack-burdened frumpish man, bespectacled and potbellied in a cheap nylon jacket and unlovely ski cap, pretending to drink from a half-empty plastic bottle of orange soda.

FIVE HOURS EAST OF WILLCOX he made camp at the edge of a shallow arroyo two hundred yards from the Interstate. It took a half hour to get his bicycle and gear over a tightly strung barbed-wire fence and across a dense swath of barbed brush, and he did the last of his chores in the dark wearing his headlamp set on low. He had just enough water to cook spaghetti and wash and make coffee in the morning, and about six ounces of sports drink.

He walked for a while in the soft sand of the arroyo. He watched a waxing gibbous moon rise over a mesa and played a few beginner's notes on his harmonica, wondering how many such nights it would take to be as good as his father had been. He tucked into his bag and woke an hour later from a dream about flat tires.

THE GATE TO THE OLD CEMETERY at Steins, New Mexico, stood open as if to suggest not negligence or invitation, but a recent exit. There was a wreath of sun-faded plastic flowers wired crookedly to the hinged barrier of chain link. He entered the little latter-day necropolis and latched the gate behind him.

There appeared at first to be about thirty mounds and markers in the rectangular half acre, but as he walked the yard in a counterclockwise tour he realized that so much of it was in ruins there was probably twice that number. Many of the plots were outlined by rotting boards on the ground. Some markers were little more than concrete rubble clinging stubbornly to rusty rebar. A half dozen graves near the entrance were topped with horizontal concrete slabs hand scratched while curing with names, dates, parting words in Spanish, crosses. An anonymous mound was distinguished by a pile of rocks and a beer bottle; another by a mature cluster of purple-and-green prickly pear.

Skeletal outgrowths of ocotillo complimented the setting in a way that made the place feel as if it had many years ago achieved whatever ambiance settles in after forlornness. The noonday sun, even in February, seemed to stamp all of it into a two-dimensional imprint on the easy north-facing hillside.

He appreciated the site for its desolation, for its solitude, for the stages through which it must have passed to become what now remained. He said hello to a duet of circling glossy ravens, to Kate and Mary and Vera and two Henrys among a cluster of restored memorials along the eastern fence, to the unnamed and unvisited.

He straightened the wreath and rewired it to the gate, then returned to his bicycle, drank half of a liter bottle of warm water, plucked burrs from his socks and a stone from one of his shoe cleats, and stood the pedals to the top of the Interstate onramp. He stopped and looked back at the cemetery: it seemed considerably farther away than a few hundred feet across a shrub-speckled vale, as if it had hunkered down in the sun to await the next passerby.

Four

The north-south line of the Rio Grande represented to Renati not only a geographic crossing point, but a planned rest from forward motion and at least a full day of equipment maintenance. He arrived early at a Las Cruces hotel and enjoyed a hot bath, supper at his favorite chain restaurant, and half of a science-fiction movie before falling asleep in a comfortable bed. He washed his clothes in a machine, sewed a tear in his windbreaker, and reviewed his maps. He inspected his bicycle fore to aft, retorquing every fastener and lubricating every moving part. He applied leather dressing to the underside of his saddle, then raised it a quarter inch and moved it forward almost as much. He added a second wrap of cork tape to the area behind the brake hoods where his palms had compressed and polished the first winding, and, after extracting from his rear tire what he hoped would be the last flat-inducing strand of retread cable, installed the inner-tube protectors he ordered in Tucson and had shipped ahead.

He marveled at what passed for entertainment on television – he had lived without a TV for eighteen years – and at what apparently constituted effective advertising. He wrote a few letters. He walked a mile and a half in the sun to an outdoor market and found at the far end an animal shelter's offering of dogs for adoption, and he spent almost an hour observing introductions and interactions. A dark-skinned girl with a mane of black hair frolicked in the blocked-off street with a clumsy mastiff puppy. When he asked if she was going to take the dog home she said, "I can't. But I play with him on Saturdays."

While returning to his hotel by way of quiet residential streets, he took from his wallet a photograph of Ragnar and sang to it the ballad Red Foley wrote about his boyhood dog. His gear was ready, his panniers packed. He felt rested. He would decide tomorrow at breakfast whether to spend the day riding or reading.

THE WOMAN WAS FAIR-COMPLECTED and delicate-featured, attired in loose blue jeans and an oversize beige sweater. Her shoulder-length brown hair was tinged lightly with gray. The moment she took her seat at the restaurant's only unoccupied table she began to hum four pairs of eighth notes – GG EE AA EE – over and over. Heads turned to stare but she seemed not to notice while her male companion perused the menu in silence. When he reached across the table and touched her gently on the shoulder and asked if she wanted buttermilk pancakes, she stopped humming long enough to reply, "Yes, please," then returned to her tune.

Renati pushed his empty plate forward and sipped the last of his coffee. His waiter delivered his bill and about-faced to take the couple's order. When he returned with two glasses of orange juice, the woman enthusiastically began tapping the heels of her flat shoes against the tiled floor in time with every other hummed note. When she began drumming the table with her palms the man reached across and slipped his hands under hers. They wore matching silver bands on their left ring fingers.

She clasped his hands and nodded and grew still, then sat a little straighter in her wooden chair. She turned slightly to face the nearest table – Renati's – and stopped humming.

He told her quietly, "The buttermilk pancakes are delicious."

She looked away and resumed her melody as if she hadn't heard, but her husband turned in his chair and, meeting Renati's gaze, offered a kindly smile. Renati recalled a verse from Dan Fogelberg's "Same Auld Lang Syne," and in that moment realized that what he saw in the man's eyes was neither doubt nor gratitude, but the truest meaning of a kept promise.

He rose and paid his bill and returned to his room, then dressed hurriedly in cycling clothes and started for Texas.

HE WAS AWARE OF HIS TENDENCY to push too hard too soon after time off the bicycle, but the adjustments he had made to his saddle, handlebars, and shoe cleats felt too good to resist. And the day was glorious! He flew past pecan groves, cotton fields, plowed ground, and over an arid Rio Grande. Past ochre adobe walls, doves on power lines, and slow-burning piles of tree slash. Where the pavement became coarse he rode the smoother painted line. Where a curve directed him into a headwind he descended to the drops and let his quadriceps burn. He hummed four pairs of eighth notes – GG EE AA EE – over and over.

Seventy minutes south of Las Cruces a primer-gray mid-1980s Cadillac forced him off the road.

He had observed the car in his mirror as it approached from several hundred yards back. There was no oncoming traffic, and no road shoulder. When it seemed certain the driver was not going to give him space, Renati hugged the uneven edge of the asphalt, unclipped his left foot from the pedal, and coasted. When no margin remained he unweighted his saddle and absorbed the six-inch drop from asphalt to sand, riding the last of his momentum into a weedy drainage channel and coming to an unsteady upright stop.

The car sped by – Texas plates on lowered suspension – with two bare arms raised high through open windows on either side, each displaying an extended middle finger. Renati half pushed, half carried his bicycle back to the pavement. He walked it for a while then crossed the road to a firm turnout and laid it on its side. He spun both wheels to check for burrs and true, then dampened a rag from his tool kit and wiped the machined braking surface of his rims. He drank a pint of water and ate a handful of banana chips and remounted.

In Canutillo forty-five minutes later he saw the Cadillac parked at the edge of a vacant gravel lot beside a liquor store.

Five

He eased off the pedals and coasted past the store. He noted an older dusty foreign car in the parking lot and a border-patrol pickup parked on the opposite side of the road, both empty. He turned right into the first side street after the store.

The Cadillac was a two-door Coupe de Ville backed against a low chain-link fence beside a dumpster on the driver's side. Both sun visors were down; only the driver was in the car. Renati unbuckled his helmet strap and twisted his left foot out of the pedal and extended his leg, stretching it to the front and side and then rearward over the pannier and back to the front. He reclipped his shoe and repeated the motion with his right leg.

He considered the damage his bicycle could have sustained had the ditch been deeper or filled with riprap. He considered the possibility that the Cadillac's owner kept in the glove box something other than the usual detritus. He banked right at the next street, hung his helmet over the bridge of his aerobars, unzipped his handlebar bag, and made another right, still coasting. Halfway down the block the dumpster came into view, then the front end of the Cadillac.

He glided to the near side of the dumpster with just enough crank rotation to silence the ticking gear cassette. He dismounted, folded his sunglasses into his handlebar bag and left the lid open, then quickly and quietly wheeled Rocinante around the rust-red bin and leaned him there and set the parking brake and stood beside the driver's door. The window was down. The driver was asleep, his head lolling to one side, his mouth open.

He was in his late twenties, Renati thought, but he looked like a huge kid. His broad brown face was soft, further softened by a sparse growth of chin beard. His black hair was buzzed close over his ears. The car was littered with fast-food trash and crumpled aluminum cans. The glove-compartment door was held shut by a frayed length of gray duct tape. Renati reached through the window and over the steering column and extracted a loop of lightweight cable strung with six or seven keys. He took a half step back and tossed the jingly cluster onto the roof.

The man's eyes opened. He glanced to his right as if at a passenger, then at Renati, and blinked. "What the fuck –" he began. His voice was low and thick. His eyes went to the bicycle and recognition dawned.

"Get out of the car," Renati said.

For a moment the man seemed confused, then he made a grab with his right hand for the ignition switch. Renati leaned forward and opened the heavy door. It bumped against the dumpster wall.

"You speak English," Renati said.

The man nodded as if he wasn't sure.

"Good. I want you to get out of the car and answer a question."

"Answer . . . ?" the man repeated.

"A question."

The man glanced again at the empty passenger seat.

"Now," Renati said.

The man mumbled something Renati could not understand, gripped the steering wheel and pivoted and put one foot, then the other, on the ground. He reached with his left hand for the grab strap on the door and pulled himself to a standing position in the narrow space. He was barrel-chested and two or three inches taller than Renati's five-eleven, but in his untucked T-shirt and sagging calf-length shorts he still looked like a big kid.

"Why did you run me off the road?" Renati asked.

The man's dull expression remained unchanged, but his eyes narrowed. Renati waited.

"What do you mean?" the man ventured after a while.

"I mean," Renati said with emphasis, "what was your reason for running me off the road?"

The big face was unaffected by clarification.

"No reason. I guess."

Renati suddenly regretted his interrupted momentum. He looked at the large hand draped limply over the door panel, and at the symbol tattooed in blue-green ink between its thumb and forefinger.

"Do you know why I stopped when I saw your car?" he asked.

The man peered past Renati toward the street. "Cuz you were pissed?" he tried.

"No," Renati said, hearing behind him only the sound of vehicles on the main road. "I stopped to punish you and your friend for assaulting me. Where is your friend? Never mind. I'm going to offer you a deal."

"A deal?" The man's eyes narrowed again.

"Yes. Promise me that you'll never run another bicyclist off the road, and I won't break the first two fingers of your left hand."

The man withdrew his hand from the door and pushed it into the pocket of his shorts.

"That won't help," Renati said.

"Okay."

"Okay, what?"

"I promise."

"You promise what? Say it."

The man looked again over Renati's shoulder. "Never to run a biker off the road."

"*Bicyclist*," Renati corrected.

"Okay."

Renati reached over the windshield, scooped the keys off the roof, and suspended them between two fingers chest high in front of the man.

"Take them," he said.

The man pulled his hand from his pocket but left it hanging at his side.

"Take them," Renati repeated. "We have a deal."

He dropped the keys into the extended palm, took a step back, slid his brake strap off the left lever with his thumb, walked his bicycle to the road and mounted and pushed away. Under a streetlamp pole two blocks south he dismounted and donned his helmet and sunglasses. He zippered the lid of his handlebar bag and drank some water and ate a few dried apricots. No one emerged from the street by the liquor store, and after a while he continued toward El Paso in a breakdown lane glittering with an extraordinary quantity and variety of broken glass.

He wished he could name what he felt. Disappointed? Cheated? Mystified? Or was it only the dull remorse he always felt after an unproductive effort?

Maybe he shouldn't have bothered. Maybe he needed a new set of rules.

He swerved into the parking lot of an out-of-business tire store and braked to a hard stop. Straddling his top tube, he pulled his music player from his handlebar bag and fitted the headphones under his helmet brim. He prompted the player and dropped it into his jersey pocket and remounted and returned at speed to the breakdown lane. To McLean, Mitchell, Debussy, and Supertramp he dodged little blue squares of safety glass, amber bottle splinters, flattened aluminum cans, a twisted wire hanger, crushed pink-framed sunglasses, a silver key, bits of shattered mirror, broken green glass stuck to a torn rectangle of paper, half of a rubber tie down, a scattering of drywall screws.

He felt better. All he needed was good music.

Six

It was a Monday night in early April, cold and snowy. He had accompanied Ragnar on an easy forest walk Saturday afternoon, but on Sunday morning the big Rhodesian ridgeback was unable to keep his balance when standing, and by afternoon he was unable to stand. Renati rolled him to the cabin in a comforter-lined garden cart and carried him up the massive stone steps and placed him in his bed by the wood stove. He made for himself a pallet on the floor and held the dog's right forepaw through the night, rising hourly to offer him water. Great soulful eyes followed his every gesture and step. By sunup the dog for whom running was life could no longer move his hind legs. By sundown his breathing had become labored. He cast frequent glances toward the door.

Twice Renati had asked his veterinarian – a large-animal specialist who made calls to area ranches – to come to his remote property when Ragnar needed help; twice the man had apologetically declined. When Renati offered five times the standard fee and round-trip transportation the veterinarian agreed, provided Renati schedule an appointment two weeks in advance.

He trudged through the snow up the hill to his office trailer, opened his desk's top-right drawer, and removed its sole contents. He checked for the always-chambered round, then extracted the magazine into his left palm and passed his thumb eighteen times over the top of it until there was a puddle of brass in the middle of the desk. He reinstalled the magazine and placed the lightened pistol into his coat pocket and walked back to the cabin.

He fashioned a nest of blankets in the deepening snow under the aspen he had transplanted a decade earlier, then opened the door and knelt beside Ragnar and stroked his side.

"I promised I would wait for you," he said. "I promised I would be with you when you were ready to say goodbye."

He slid his arms beneath the cedar-shavings mattress and stood and carried the drooping bundle outside and placed it gently into the soft circlet. He lay in the snow behind his dog, cradling him between his chest and knees. Against a velvety ear he talked about running and eating and going for rides in the truck. He talked about their feline friends, Kira and Gobi and Sahara. He reminded him of the time he treed a black bear and stopped a charging cow moose and chased a gray wolf and had to be rescued from a pack of coyotes. He told him he was sorry for not always understanding him. He told him he was the best dog in the world and that he loved him and he held him close and kissed the top of his handsome head and placed the muzzle of his pistol where his lips had been and pulled the trigger.

Falling snow had a way of intensifying stillness and muffling silence, particularly in the dark. Renati's screams did not travel far.

AS HE JOINED THE INTERSTATE southeast of Fort Hancock he felt the familiar gusty pressure of tractor-trailer wind nudging him forward. He had taken an extra day in Clint to avoid freezing rain above Sierra Blanca, and used the time to write letters. The sixty miles to Van Horn would mark the end of his Interstate-highway pedaling.

His knee seldom hurt, his saddle leather was properly conditioned, and he hadn't had a flat in over a hundred miles. He discerned no increase in rolling resistance after installing tire liners, although on a heavy rig with constantly changing surfaces it was hard to be sure. He had begun to experience discomfort, like a cramp or a bruise, in his left heel, but it only bothered him when he walked. His Las Cruces handlebar and saddle adjustments appreciably mitigated the finger tingling that kept him ever varying grip positions. He recollected having numb hands on long rides in his youth, but fifteen years of working with chainsaws, drawknives, chisels, and mallets had made deadened digits a routine inconvenience to be shaken off.

He wondered when he would face a headwind strong enough to balance the accomplice so often at his back. Probably, he thought, at a time when he would not credit it as a balancing. The only rain he had felt since leaving Chula Vista was a sprinkle one night while walking to a store.

Compared to temperatures behind him, the air above Sierra Blanca was frigid. He zipped his nylon windbreaker over his sweater, then donned his leg warmers and cap and, for the first time, long-fingered gloves. Although he had been raised where winters were bitter and had in his first profession pursued snow wherever it accumulated, for the past three years he had felt the cold in a manner wholly anomalous. Gone, it seemed, was the internal core of heat that had so reliably kept him comfortable when outdoors in arctic conditions.

He wondered if his attraction to the desert was due as much to its permeating warmth as to its desolation.

Lost in thought and overflowing with the energy that often coursed through his body a few hours before sundown, he rode two miles past his exit with a long shadow stretched before him.

"That's one way," he said to Rocinante, "to turn a tailwind into a headwind."

His heel ache was making him angry. He was certain he had not bruised it and it scarcely hurt when pedaling, but even short walks made it feel as if someone had thumped it with a hammer. Between riding and writing he had neglected stretching; his leg muscles were no longer hard, but they still would not relax. Probably there was a connection.

He booked a room in Van Horn for two days' rest. A cold front with icy winds set in, and two days became five. He met a woman whose marriage had ended in a way that left her alone with a teenage son and a question Renati recognized but had been unable to put into words.

How do you remember a life that was not what it seemed?

Seven

South of Valentine, Renati turned left on Ranch to Market 505, square into his overdue headwind. He was already exhausted from leaning into a forceful easterly for three hours, and an additional fifty minutes in low gears yielded only five miles through country where there was insufficient cover to conceal his camp. With less than an hour of daylight remaining he spotted what appeared to be a dip in the ground two hundred yards up a gentle hillside south of the road. A ranch gate piled high with tumbleweeds barred admittance to a pair of ruts that snaked their way to within fifty yards of the grassy depression. He donned his windbreaker and cleared enough of the prickly blockage to open the gate the width of his panniers. He closed and chained it behind him and quickly pushed his ride up the grade to what he hoped would be an adequate spot to spend the night.

It was ideal: a rectangular basin beside an excavated pile of grown-over topsoil. The grass in the thirty-inch-deep hollow was long and soft, and after extracting a few thorny dead branches he staked out his ground cloth and erected his house and inflated his mattress and ate a cold supper of tortillas, canned oysters, and dried pineapple.

IN THE MORNING he was awakened by a covey of clucking birds uphill from his tent. He had slept eleven hours. The day was so beautiful and his coffee and banana and granola cereal so satisfying he contemplated staying a while. He was far enough from the road to be undisturbed by the sparse traffic; he had just enough water and food for another day; Fort Davis was not quite thirty miles distant.

He took a leisurely exploratory walk and was packed and peddling by noon.

It was a peaceful climb along Highway 166 into the Davis Mountains. He lunched at six thousand feet on a rock wall beside the entrance to a religious retreat called, according to the sign, Bloys Camp. Although the corrugated-steel barracks looked sufficient to house at least a thousand people and he could easily picture bustling activity, the settlement lacked even a stirring breeze. He arrived mid-afternoon at Fort Davis and pitched his tent in a campground on the main street after an hour-long conversation with the establishment's Air Force-veteran owner. He dined at a Mexican restaurant and read in his sleeping bag until his headlamp quit.

The road to Alpine was refreshingly green; the damp air was invigorating. A low gray sky hinted at rain, but none fell. He wore his sweater and knee warmers and long-fingered gloves for the first hour, riding hard up and fast down bucolic rolling hills. For the first time in four cycles of his music collection, the birdsong that introduced Supertramp's "Even in the Quietest Moments" did not rouse him to search for a singing bird.

He laughed and said, "I was starting to wonder how many times I'd fall for that!"

He was surprised to realize that he liked Texas. It was not, as he had come to think of it during many crossings by automobile, merely a vast stretch of ground to put behind him en route to someplace else. While nooning on the tracks of the Galveston, Harrisburg and San Antonio Railway he decided he might even return if the secession rumors he had heard proved to be true.

AT A CAMPGROUND IN MARATHON at one twenty in the morning two days later, a northwesterly blast of wind lifted half of his unstaked tent off the ground and dropped it so hard he bounced on his mattress. Violent gusts tore at his shelter's rain fly for the next five hours; the temperature dropped from sixty-four to twenty-nine.

He walked a mile to a breakfast restaurant and was twice blown several feet sideways. He returned to his tent ninety minutes later, broke camp, and checked into a motel. His heel pain was worsening, but since it didn't result from an injury he did his best to ignore it.

HE HAD ESTABLISHED TWO OBJECTIVES for his Texas crossing: see the remains of a movie set south of Del Rio, and visit a friend from thirty years past now residing with her husband and children northwest of San Antonio. The plan helped distract him from a nagging desire to turn south into Mexico at every border town since Yuma. Trusted ex-military friends with knowledgeable connections in Central America had, after graphically describing a scenario they considered likely, warned him from his original route through northern Mexico, but proximity to the border furnished a constant temptation to disregard their advice. His decision to pedal from the Pacific to the Atlantic and catch a boat out of Florida to Colombia was not disagreeable, but riding through Louisiana, Mississippi, Alabama, and Georgia appealed not in the least, and the closer those states loomed on his map the more longingly he fixed his gaze on the southern horizon.

He stopped for late-afternoon coffee at a one-table restaurant and gift shop on Highway 90 north of Langtry, and took a sunset detour to where the old town perched on a bluff overlooking the Rio Grande. Bristly green vegetation bordered a band of duller green in the canyon below; across the river, Coahuila was a brown-and-gray still life. He traversed the stony promontory that defined the Pump Canyon confluence, and lingered at the Langtry cemetery.

For only the second time since climbing from sea level at the Pacific he gazed upon a landscape that invited him to stay. He found it curious that both enticements were in Texas.

The sun was down by the time he returned to the main road, so he rented a rough little room behind the gift shop. He slept in his bag on unlaundered linens, ate a Mexican breakfast in the morning, made lunch east of the Pecos, and arrived in Del Rio with energy and daylight to spare. *Lonesome Dove*'s Hat Creek filming location was reportedly extant on private property west of US

277, but his inquiry to the contact he located in Illinois had not yet been answered.

IT WAS WELL AFTER DARK when he opened their Tok, Alaska, post-office box and found a package addressed to him from Little Rock, Arkansas. Inside was a gift-wrapped video cassette and a birthday card signed, "From your lonesome dove." He was weary after a thousand miles of driving and a hundred of hiking in search of land they had come north to purchase and homestead, and by the time he had finished unhitching, leveling, and utility-connecting their '77 Argosy it was after midnight and he could barely raise his arms, but he showered and pushed his gift into the player and settled against propped-up pillows to watch a few minutes of a six-hour movie he had never seen. It was dawn when he pressed *stop* and nudged Ozark the cat off the fold-out bed and turned onto his side and fell asleep.

"A man of vision, you say?" Captain Call had replied to the young newspaperman at the end of the story. "Yeah. Hell of a vision."

HE WAITED ANOTHER TWO DAYS in Del Rio but his request for permission to visit the movie set was never answered. He packed and loaded his gear, reined Rocinante toward San Antonio, and broke from the border.

Eight

Texas was abloom with blues, reds, purples, and yellows. Most creek beds were wet; some were flowing. Spring seemed months early. From a bridge east of Hondo, Renati counted nine turtles crowded on a half-sunken log in an algae-congested backwater. All but one plopped into the avocado-colored soup by the time he dismounted and walked back with his camera. He rolled two peanut-butter-and-honey tortillas while sitting on the guardrail and, in answer to a friend's request for "more selfies" – the definition of which he had found on the Internet – he snapped an arm's-length photo.

His friend, he thought, would probably not recognize him wearing a bandanna, or, had he removed it, with a shaved head.

The woman he was soon to visit in Helotes had been nine when he befriended her and her brother at the resort where he directed a summer ski camp on five chairlift-served acres of white AstroTurf. The touristy Smoky Mountains town of Gatlinburg had been his home and training headquarters for six summers over seven years. Sometimes he arrived with an automobile, sometimes with only a bicycle, but always he had a bicycle. In 1982, after a winter of unanswered questions, he traded summer on "the turf" for summer on a bicycle.

He flew from Boston to San Francisco with a white Bianchi and red Nashbar panniers, hoping that a solo ride back to his parents' home in New Hampshire would help him decide whether or not to continue his career in skiing. His Weber State College roommate collected him at the airport; two days later he rode east out of San Jose. He climbed the Sierra Nevada in a May snowstorm and spent a weekend in Reno with his friend and former archrival on the World Cup Freestyle Skiing circuit.

He crossed to Salt Lake City over Interstate 80 in five days, injuring both Achilles tendons from a saddle positioned too high. He rode out of Aspen for Leadville only to find that the warnings he ignored proved sensible: Colorado 82 was closed by snowdrifts, the second of which he could neither push his bicycle through nor carry it around. He retreated through Basalt and was offered a lift through a maze of construction on Interstate 70 by two men in a Ford Bronco. After loading his gear he introduced himself to the driver.

"I know who you are," said the man. "I photographed you at Heavenly Valley in seventy-seven."

He began the climb to Loveland Pass under a cloudless early-summer sky, but by the time he topped the summit he was in a thunder-punctuated blizzard. Back on the Interstate, after a deceptive sunshiny reprieve, he raced a white wave of roiling flakes into Georgetown and ate a cheeseburger lunch while his slush-drenched clothes dried before an enormous stone fireplace. He ignored the "NO BICYCLES" sign at the start of a side road that more or less followed Clear Creek toward Denver, and pedaled through five unlighted rock-cut tunnels.

He grew weary of Kansas and took a left into Nebraska after Norton. Not much of a change, he had to admit, except for the name. He saw *Annie* at a stately old theater with his bicycle in the aisle beside his seat, and afterward slept under a picnic table in the town park. On US 6 east of Hastings he came upon a baby skunk lying beside its mother's crushed body in the westbound lane.

The tiny creature scurried away when Renati stopped, but got only as far as the waist-high cornstalks before returning to its mother. He transferred the contents of his rack trunk to an improvised bundle over his handlebar bag, made a nest of grass, and zipped him, or her – "Pedro," anyway – in. From a farmhouse he dialed the number of an animal-rescue organization in Lincoln, and arranged with the woman who answered to meet him at four o'clock at a downtown intersection. He arrived fifteen minutes early in a bizarre darkening stillness. A few people hurriedly walked the streets; the traffic lights seemed irrelevant. At five to four a green station wagon braked to a stop in front of him and a middle-aged brown-haired woman stepped out of the car, transferred Pedro to a lidded wicker basket, said "thank you" and "you better get off the street," returned to her car and sped away. Renati thought he heard squealing tires after the vehicle was out of sight.

Across the road in front of a bicycle shop stood a red-haired girl of about twenty waving both hands over her head. He wheeled his Bianchi in her direction and called, "Where is everybody?"

The girl answered, "You can wait out the tornado in our basement."

Three days later, outfitted with puncture-resistant tubes inside better tires, rigid-shanked touring shoes, new gloves, and his first Brooks saddle, he crossed the Missouri on the Plattsmouth Bridge. A thousand miles and two weeks farther east, while waiting half-saddled in heavy rain at a T-junction near London, Ontario, he was struck from behind by a black Chevrolet Camaro. The impact propelled him across the corner of a grassy meridian, his right foot still cinched tight in a toe clip. He landed on his tucked-under right shoulder in the lane of traffic that had the green light as the Camaro ran the red and disappeared in the downpour.

He did what he could to true his rear wheel in the service bay of a nearby gas station, but had to adjust his Mavic cantilever brakes to oblige a recalcitrant wobble. With his leather belt he secured a plastic bag of ice over his right deltoid and finished his planned hundred and twenty-five mile day to the American side of Niagara Falls. After resting in the lakeside cabin of a friend, he shipped his panniers ahead and raced home on a forty-pound machine, spending the last of what was left in his wallet on restaurant meals and hotel beds.

For the next three weeks he descended daily into the basement of his parents' farmhouse and stared at his bicycle and pondered his journey and desperately missed both. He had patched seventeen flat tires in the nineteen hundred miles between San Jose and Lincoln, and not one more in the sixteen hundred that followed. His longest day – while trying to cross Illinois in a single push – was one hundred and sixty-five miles; his daily average was eighty-four. He had spent every cent of his savings, and then what his father had been able to raise by selling his van, but the moment his ride was over he knew that it had been the most beneficial departure from his particular normality that he could ever have given himself.

He returned to Gatlinburg the following summer to resume training while working nights at Pat and Don MacPherson's Sweet Fanny Adams Theatre, first as handyman and prop builder, then as sound-and-lighting technician, then as Mark Goodheart in one of their delightful musical comedies. Every other evening he clambered onto the springy saddle of the theater's refurbished pennyfarthing to pedal Parkway and River Road in early-1900s costume. Three years later, after the finest season of a decade-long calling, he retired his skis to a storage stall in his parents' barn.

Nine

He bade farewell to his friend and her family thinking that if one needed a city, San Antonio was a good choice. He had toured the Riverwalk by boat and visited Mission San José and the Alamo, savored his first Texas barbecue, read a book about "love languages," watched animated movies, and kicked a soccer ball. He had enjoyed the company of good children and devoted parents, and the opportunity to contemplate a time and place long past. His heel pain had neither decreased nor increased.

He squinted into the late-morning sun and realized that for the past fifteen hundred miles, down hills and up, whether the wind was at his back or in his face, one thought had held steadfast: he was right to ride. He wondered, smiling, what his grandfather had in mind when he penned inside Renati's high-school graduation card thirty-nine years ago, "May the road rise up to meet you."

ON HIS WAY OUT OF SAN ANTONIO, at a grocery store on the east side of the city, two men in their early twenties stood ahead of him in the checkout line. The one in front was dressed in camo-patterned baggy shorts and a hooded gray sweatshirt. The other wore a black tank top with jeans belted around his upper thighs. Between the hem of his shirt and the waistband of his pants was a six-inch display of red-and-gray-plaid boxer shorts.

Their conversation was loud and profane, clearly making the elderly couple in front of them uncomfortable. The young cashier seemed unperturbed.

Renati tapped the closer of the two on the shoulder and said,

"Your pants are falling down."

The man turned. He sported a silver bar through the skin above his left eye and a smudged tattoo under his right. He stared for a moment and said, "What the fuck is it to you?"

Renati replied, "If my pants were falling down I'd want someone to tell me."

The man looked genuinely astonished. He said to his friend, "Is this asshole serious?"

Gray Hoodie laughed. "Maybe he wants to get his ass kicked."

Renati placed his purchase on the motionless conveyor. Pants Falling Down asked, "Is that what you want?"

"I just want orange juice," Renati answered. "Although I'd rather buy it without seeing your ridiculous underwear."

The two men glanced at each other. Gray Hoodie had either a cell-phone holster or a knife sheath on his right hip under his sweatshirt. He didn't look like the sort to carry a multitool, Renati thought.

Pants Falling Down said in a low tone, "I think you really do want to get your ass kicked."

"No, I really don't," Renati said. "But pay for your . . ." He peered around the pair to see the cashier sliding a blue-and-white eighteen-pack of beer over the scanner. "Pay for your diet beverage. I'll be outside in a minute."

They were waiting in the parking lot beside a black Honda Accord on undersized wheels with preposterously incorrect offset. Renati was almost surprised not to hear rap music coming from wherever rap music comes from. He walked to his bicycle and set his orange juice on the concrete. He pulled the rubber protectors from his cleats and lifted his sunglasses from the neck of his shirt and placed them with his wallet inside his handlebar bag. A tall girl with a blonde ponytail pushed a line of shopping carts between where he stood in the shade of the building and where his new friends stood in the sun beside their car.

He called across the fifty feet that separated them: "Well?"

Gray Hoodie started forward but Pants Falling Down said something Renati couldn't hear and Hoodie stopped. Renati picked up his orange juice and unscrewed the lid, drank half, and stood the bottle back on the concrete.

Pants Falling Down again said something to his companion and then yelled to Renati, "This is your lucky day, asshole!"

Gray Hoodie turned and went to the driver's side of the car and unlocked the door. He got in and leaned across to unlock the passenger side. Pants Falling Down opened the door and hiked up his pants and sat in the seat and closed the door. Renati expected a parting gesture or comment but the car moved slowly toward the exit and entered the street.

SOUTHEAST OF SUTHERLAND SPRINGS he glimpsed a big calico cat curled in a ball in the rangy grass beside US 87. He rode another few seconds before realizing that the animal's eyes were open and dull. He checked his mirror for traffic and wheeled around and dismounted and propped Rocinante against his shock-corded parking stand. He waved away flies and lifted the furry torus and carried it to a shady spot under a tree beside a stone wall. The flattened grass where the creature had lain was dark with dried blood. He rinsed his hands under a water-bottle stream and shook them dry, then walked with his bicycle across the road toward a small white-clapboarded house at the end of a long gravel driveway. He rapped on the wooden frame of a rusty screen door.

The woman who greeted him from behind the screen didn't know who owned the cat, so he returned to the highway, bade adieu to the feline, and continued toward Stockdale. A few miles down Texas 119 he found on the narrow shoulder a saw-toothed shedding blade like the one he had used for grooming Ragnar. He glanced at the date window on his watch. He pulled his cell phone from his handlebar bag and double-checked the number.

He laughed, shaking his head. It was Ragnar's birthday.

He wedged the blade in the elastic webbing over his pantry bag, and a couple of hours later braked in front of an expansive house sited eighty yards downhill from the road. On freshly mowed grass behind a gated high fence, three large short-hair dogs enthusiastically competed in a barking-and-running contest.

He hooked the tool over one of the gate's pointy tines, waved to the aproned white-haired woman staring at him from an open porch on the side of the house, searched his music player for an energy boost, then clipped in and pushed off to the Outlaws' version of "Riders in the Sky."

Taking the lead a few feet ahead, smiling a great dog smile, Ragnar glanced back every few seconds to be sure his pal was keeping pace. His floppy big ears floated rhythmically up and down with every distance-consuming leap, the dark ridge on his back a skimming arrow. At the top of a low rise at the top of his voice, elongating both syllables as had been his habit on the mountain, Renati cried:

"Raaaagnaaaar..."

HE WAS INHALING FAINTLY SALTY AIR east of Lake Texana when an idea began to form – an idea that did not feature New Orleans, Biloxi, or Mobile. He checked into a Bay City hotel and examined his printed maps, then went online to view the roads connecting Mexico with Panama. He compared his Galveston to-do list with his calendar, and his calendar with weather averages for south of the Tropic of Cancer in May and June. He had never enjoyed working or riding in heat and humidity, but, he thought, what better way to contemplate life in Central America than during the season he knew would be his least favorite? He could parallel the Gulf and then cross to the Pacific in Nicaragua, steering clear of San Pedro Sula, Guatemala City, Managua, El Salvador. The more he studied the option, the more he liked the line of it: Chula Vista to Galveston, Galveston to Cancun by water if possible and by air if not, Cancun to El Porvenir, then by sailboat through the San Blas Islands to Cartagena in time for his fifty-seventh birthday.

He rose early, had an all-day breakfast, and was pedaling soon after what would have been sunup if it was not so darkly overcast. He said good morning to dogs and crows and children waiting for school buses, and to his shadow when it appeared for a few seconds. He practiced "good morning" in Spanish and "how are you?" and "I am well." He ate nuts and dried fruit near the creek where he had planned to camp, then remounted and rode without stopping another twenty miles to a hotel in Alvin.

That night, after watching *Hero at Large* from his computer library, he dreamed of a July afternoon near the summit of Red Mountain when his speech failed, his vision turned to oscilloscope undulations, and he felt a pressure in his skull the likes of which he had never before experienced. As his wife and their two hiking companions hurried him down the steep trail, he knew that only one thing mattered if only minutes were left to him. He stopped. He turned his wife to meet his increasingly unclear gaze, struggling to compose in his increasingly unclear mind the words he needed to express what their life together meant to him.

He said, "I . . . likey . . . you."

HE DELAYED FOR A THUNDERSTORM he preferred not to confront when crossing the causeway bridge to Galveston, and early the next afternoon arrived at the Beachcomber Inn. He took a five-mile stroll along the seawall, partly because it promised to be a splendid evening and partly to spite his heel. He consumed a few thousand calories at a Chinese buffet, stopped at a grocery store for a jug of good orange juice, and returned to his room to spread maps, notes, and lists across the spare bed.

An entrepreneur and disaster-recovery specialist he met at a thrift store in Arizona had recommended a three-target approach to the acquisition of distant goals. A ten-meter target, his new friend explained, educates and motivates, serving to bring a more-remote objective, a hundred-meter target, into range. With the knowledge, momentum, and commitment earned while acquiring a hundred-meter target, a thousand-meter target becomes achievable.

The road to Galveston was Renati's ten-meter target. Before him, arrayed like a collage over a colorful flowery bedspread, was his hundred-meter target. Once he became what he needed to be – a stranger navigating strange lands under his own power – his thousand-meter target would come into view.

Or so he believed.

Along the Way

Chula Vista . . . Galveston

One

MR and Ragnar

Rocinante at San Diego Bay

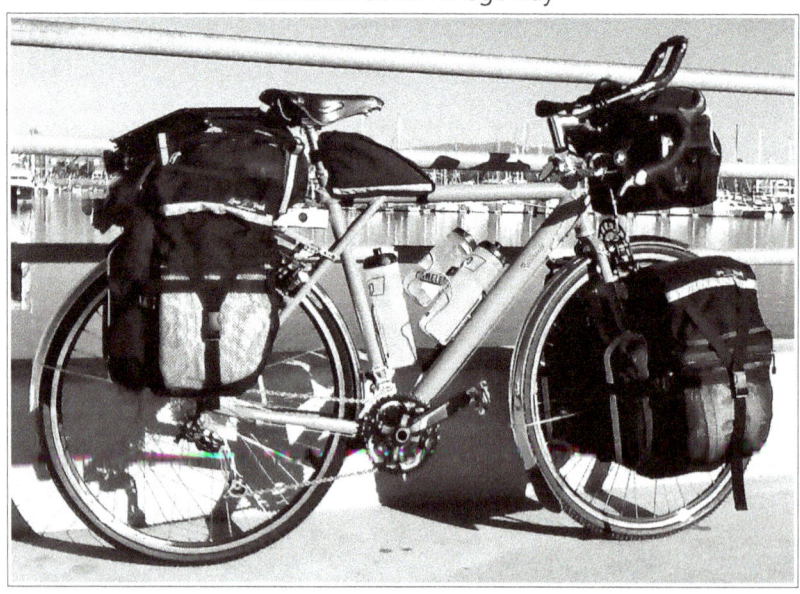

One night by a stream

A cabin in the Montana Rockies

Under stars and helicopters

"There was an ol' tin cup, a battered ol' coffee pot . . ."

Campo Road west of Diabold Canyon

Preparing for a pilot-truck ride through construction

Everything

Confirming wheel-build quality north of Nuevo Algodones

Two

Rocinante's "condition as a hack before he became . . .

. . . the first and foremost of all the hacks in the world."

A Baja California Norte trial three years earlier

Sans panniers north of Puertocitos, same ride

Fifty miles overland to Mexico

From the perspective of a tailwind

For Joni Mitchell

A sunset exit for Casa Grande . . . to be continued tomorrow

Three

Arroyo real estate east of Willcox

Rocinante at rest

The self-elevating method of roadside flat repair

Found it!

Descansa en paz

Across the four-lane trail from the cemetery

Four

Descending into Las Cruces

Hoping for home

Five

Winter pecans

A parched Rio Grande south of Mesilla

Bike

Bikes

Bicycle

Six

He stopped a charging moose and befriended a baby robin

Copilots

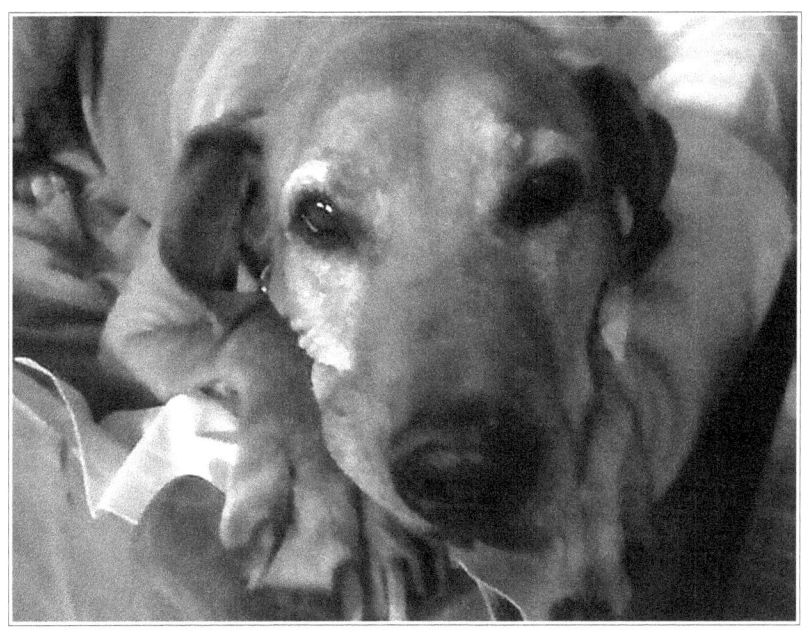

Happy eighty-fourth birthday!

A common Van Horn aesthetic

Writing in the park after the cold front passed

Seven

Calling it a day in a perfect setting

A lovely climb into the Davis Mountains

Bloy's Camp

Arkady Renko knows the feeling

Lunch on the Galveston, Harrisburg and San Antonio

The Rio Grande at Langtry

Eight

Snowdance, 1975 – 1985 (Richard Russell photos)

East of Denver, 1982 (Kevin Dunn photo)

Nine

For want of a short-haired dog

A lunch companion at Lake Texana

There is no such thing as too many bicycle pictures

Crossing West Bay to Galveston

STAGE TWO

Stranger in a Strange Land

To sing, to laugh, to dream,
to walk in my own way and be alone,
free, with an eye to see things as they are,
a voice that means manhood. To cock my hat
where I choose. At a word – a yes, a no, to fight or write.
To travel any road under the sun, under the stars, nor
care if fame or fortune lie beyond the bourne.
Never to make a line I have not heard in my
own heart; yet, with all modesty to say:

"My soul, be satisfied with flowers,
with fruit, with weeds even; but gather them in
the one garden you may call your own."

Cyrano de Bergerac
Edmond Rostand, 1898

Ten

The stench of smoldering garbage burned Renati's nostrils; exhaust fumes stung his eyes. The air was so hot and the humidity so extreme he found himself laughing at the absurdity of it. An hour south of his hotel on the shore of Cancún's Laguna Nichupté, he coasted to a stop in a narrow band of shade beneath a steel-framed pedestrian overpass.

I'm breathing agua caliente, he thought.

His head hurt directly behind his eyes. He felt dizzy and slightly nauseated. He grabbed a water bottle and pulled the nozzle open between his teeth and squeezed and drank. The liquid was warmer than the inside of his mouth. He swallowed the full liter of it, closed the nozzle with his forefinger, and pushed the empty back into the lower cage on his down tube.

His cyclometer showed thirty-six degrees Celsius. Thirty-six times five divided by nine plus – or was it times nine divided by five plus thirty-two? He wondered idly how long it would take to think in centigrade and kilometers.

He hooked his helmet onto his aerobars and peeled the sodden liner from his skull. He grabbed his emergency satellite texting device from his handlebar bag and his lunch from his pantry bag. Strawberry yogurt plus a peanut-butter-and-honey tortilla plus thirty minutes in the shade, he decided, would help. He stood his bicycle against his parking stand and grabbed a second bottle from the seat-tube cage, then ascended the pedestrian ramp to where the railing began and jumped lightly to the ground on the side opposite the road.

His left foot twisted a bit in the loose gravel and he felt an odd twitch in his lower shin. He made a picnic spot on a dusty concrete footing, sent a promised test message from his emergency satellite texting device to his brother in New Hampshire, peeled back the foil lid of his yogurt cup, and dipped his camp spoon into the runny pink pudding.

He was pleased with his new equipment. The glass in his accessory-bar-mounted rear-view mirror had cracked during the flight from Houston, but the German-made replacement he ordered from a store in Oregon was an improvement and would be, he already knew, an ally on Mexican and Central American roads. His new shoes were good. His new helmet and liner and gloves and socks were good. His new tires were a special kind of good: on flat terrain it felt like he was rolling slightly downhill, as if an acceleration compound had been molded into the rubber.

All of his upgrades were good, but being a stranger in a strange land was already *great*.

He poured the entirety of water-bottle two down his throat and felt the rivulets of sweat on his forearm change direction. He longed for a drink he could *feel*. His brother replied.

"Are you okay?" he asked Rocinante.

NEVER BEFORE HAD HE WISHED he did not have a tailwind. He experienced the relief of a breeze only when he stopped, otherwise his pace matched the southerly wind's speed so closely he felt as if he was riding in a bubble of heated stillness. His headache had lessened and his nausea had passed, but a mild vertigo wafted like ripples on the verge of his concentration. He had stopped twice for cold beverages – a quart of orange juice first, a quart of chocolate milk an hour later. Probably they didn't mix very well, he thought, but orange juice and chocolate milk were what called to him, and he could feel their restorative chill when he swallowed. The refrigerated yellow sports beverage with which he had filled two of his bottles had long since stopped dripping condensation and was now as hot as the air.

At two o'clock he found himself paralleling a lush carpet of freshly trimmed grass in front of a three-meter-high adobe wall. He unclipped his shoes and braked gently to a stop and helped his rig over a low curb and leaned it against one of a trio of mature palms. He dropped his helmet beside his bicycle and pulled his gloves inside out and stretched on his back in the shade of the wall. He needed another drink but the bottles were too far away. He closed his eyes.

His transition from restful thoughts to sleeping dreams was halted by a sudden hissing, like air through a depressed tire valve. The instant he raised his head he was hit squarely in the face by a jet of lukewarm water, and he heard all around him the pulsing tssst-tssst-tssst of oscillating irrigation sprinklers. He laughed, stood, wheeled his bicycle to a triangular island of brittle brown grass and laid it down, removed his shoes and socks, and returned barefoot to sit where he had almost fallen asleep. Within a minute he was drenched. A few minutes later the sprinklers quit and dropped like little brass gophers into their holes.

He wrung the water from his shirt and gloves and donned his socks and shoes and slipped back into the tailwind, a little faster, perhaps, than before. He arrived at Playa del Carmen in time to shower and dress and relax with a sunset walk to an excellent pasta supper at an Italian restaurant on La Quinta Avenida.

THE NEXT MORNING the muscles along the outside of his left shin, a palm's width above his ankle, were strangely tight. He stretched the area gently before breakfast, then massaged and stretched it again after breakfast. There was no swelling, no discoloration, no reason for stiffness. He swapped his wool anklets for mid-calf synthetic compression socks, made three trips with his gear down a wide tiled stairway, and in the hotel's tropical garden attached panniers to racks beside a life-size buxom Mayan female immortalized in a naked gymnastic back bend in the basin of a concrete fountain.

He checked his watch: barely nine o'clock and already he felt overheated. He dried his face and arms with the microfiber towel he kept under his pantry-bag webbing. He drank a half bottle of air-conditioner-cooled bluish sports beverage. He said *gracias* to the hotel manager, pedaled Calle 1 Sur to Carretera Federal 307, and rejoined the tailwind.

GALVESTON HAD PERFECTLY SUITED his rest from Stage One while he prepared for Stage Two. His days began with the Beachcomber Inn's continental breakfast. He ate peanut butter and jelly on bakery bread for lunch and had a light grocery-deli meal most nights. He shopped online for a better helmet and tires, new shoes, socks, gloves, shorts, and street pants. He bought a digital voice recorder and, after totaling the cost of mailing books to Central and South America from his one-box library in Arizona, an electronic reader smaller and only slightly heavier than the paperback that was always in his handlebar bag. The hotel office received nearly two dozen packages during his stay; he frequented a nearby mailbox store to return the gear that didn't meet his expectations and to ship what he sold online.

The plastic stiffeners inside his otherwise-excellent panniers had deformed – a couple thousand miles too soon, he thought – causing a slouchy appearance and tangential strain on the fasteners. He purchased four feet of quarter-by-two-inch aluminum bar, a cheap corded drill, a hacksaw, and a file larger than the four he carried, then reconstructed the bags the way they should have been made originally. The project added twenty-eight ounces to his ride but the result rode proudly and the bags' lifespan would be tripled. He borrowed a bench grinder to shorten the tapered aluminum bushing between front fender and fork crown, increasing tire clearance from eight to eleven millimeters.

Except for rides to test upgraded equipment, he walked where he needed to go and took long meanders at night along the seawall. Gradually the pain in his heel faded and disappeared. Plantar fasciitis, he suspected.

He wrote letters, read the first six chapters of Benjamin Franklin's autobiography, reviewed his scanned handwritten notes from Ian Hibbel's *Into the Remote Places* and the Darien Gap hostage debacle *Cloud Garden*, pored over maps of Mexico and Central America, and composed in his journal.

The arched hollow lid of his handlebar bag carried his three identical music players, each powered – like his camera, flashlight, taillight, headlamp, digital recorder, and hair clippers – by AA batteries charged with a compact folding solar panel. Into the first player he transferred two hours of new music; into the second he added Martin Cruz Smith's *Red Square* to Elizabeth Peters' *The Deeds of the Disturber* and Cormac McCarthy's *Cities of the Plain*. He assigned to the third a program of Spanish lessons entertainingly Scottish-accented.

He inquired locally about catching a boat to the Yucatán, but the cost was high and availability uncertain. He reconsidered the counsel of his ex-military friends and found that two of their warned-off regions were between him and where he wanted to go. He would have ignored the State Department's paranoid advisories, but he trusted his friends and booked a one-way flight to Cancún out of Houston.

He ordered a pair of canvas duffel bags for transporting his panniers, and constructed for his bicycle a crate out of heavy corrugated cardboard, one-by-eight pine, and swivel casters. He measured and weighed the finished product: five inches and sixteen pounds shy of the airline's maximum. He stared contemplatively at the more vulnerable parts of his machine, then twenty minutes later at department-store bedding-display shelves. He returned to his room carrying a cheap fleece blanket and so many pillows under his arms he had to step off the sidewalk every time he met a pedestrian. He smoothed the blanket around the frame and fitted the pillows, still in their packaging, into every empty space. He cinched the duffel bags lengthwise to the top of the crate with nylon tie-downs, then rolled the contraption into the hotel parking lot for a practice run.

It was a cool evening, cloudless and breezy and possibly his last in the country of his birth. Beyond the cone-shaped glare of parking-lot lights, somewhere over the states through which he preferred not to ride, a new moon was ascending.

Eighteen hours later, with an ebullience that belied his wakeful night and pre-dawn embarkation, he was striding purposefully through the corridors of Aeropuerto Internacional de Cancún. Gliding effortlessly beside him, Rocinante's boxcar rhythmically tick-ticked over marble tiles.

"START," HE SAID into the microphone clipped to the open neck of his jersey. "Testing, one, two, three," he continued. "This is speaking directly ahead. Testing, testing. This is speaking downward at the mic. Testing, testing, four, five, six. Speaking downward is uncomfortable and limits my view of the road, so I hope it sounds okay straight ahead. Thirty kilometers per hour going slightly downhill, about a twenty-five-K tailwind, lots of passing traffic. These kilometer markers are encouraging." He chuckled. "They go by so fast!"

He positioned his right index finger over the recorder's stop button and said, "End."

Eleven

It wasn't the fifteen-minute queue at the Tulum-ruins ticket window that persuaded Renati to forego a tour, it was the clamorous party atmosphere that pervaded the scene. He had intended to backtrack to the site from his hotel in the morning, but when he passed the turnoff five hours before sundown he decided not to wait.

Visitors clad in tourist-store shirts and every conceivable size of swimwear milled about the park entrance clutching brochures, cameras, beverages, and beach towels. Children darting to and fro trailed string-tied bobbing blue balloons. Competing conversations in English, Spanish, and German bordered on raucous and the tableau, he thought, was better suited to carnival amusement than to archaeological insight.

He found a place to rest between tourists sitting on a white-painted masonry wall in front of the ticket office. He gripped Rocinante's top tube with one hand while freeing a water bottle with the other. A short man wearing a blue-and-white uniform told him he had to move his bicycle, pointing in the direction of a welded-steel rack jammed with creaky-looking relics.

"*Por ahí*," he added.

Renati nodded and raised his bottle. The man stood a little taller and planted his hands on his hips.

"Okay," Renati said.

He slipped the bottle back into its cage and mounted and coasted, feet free of the pedals, a few hundred meters down a tree-lined lane to a stone-and-mortar wall. He ate a couple of chewy granola bars while watching a big iguana watching him. He proffered a bite between extended fingers and the reptile disappeared behind a log. It began to rain. The muscles at the front of his left shin felt slightly tender.

HE WOKE AT FOUR IN THE MORNING and sat naked at the edge of his bed. The air conditioner was blowing tepid air. His mind was hazy, still clinging to sleep. He knew he had been dreaming but couldn't remember about what. In the yellow haze of the hotel's courtyard lights he confirmed an obstacle-free path to the bathroom, stood, took one step, and collapsed onto his right knee.

He remained motionless for a moment, then cautiously straightened his left foot. Shifting his weight and leaning against the bed, he rose over his right leg and sat, straddling the corner of the mattress.

"Ow," he said.

Twelve

He had eaten his free breakfast – two miniature cartons of peach juice and a child-size plastic pouch of instant cereal – the night before. His coffee press stood inverted on a paper towel beside the kitchenette sink. His titanium mug, two-thirds full of a savory granola mix from a store in Cancún, leaned by his right thigh where he sat propped against a pair of lumpy pillows between his back and the blue concrete wall behind his mattress. A third pillow, covered with a patterned-orange slipcase that smelled of something unpleasant and that had spent the night on the floor, now elevated his left leg beneath a tissue-thin sheet pulled to his waist. A plastic tortilla bag containing what little frost he had been able to scrape from the mini-fridge lay draped over his left shin. The air conditioner continued its feckless exhalation.

His slender black steel pen, designed to write upside-down, under water, and in zero gravity – two scenarios of which he had tested and confirmed – moved and paused and moved across the tan clothbound journal in his lap. He wrote:

> *Art as beautification, as condemnation*
>
> *Bad behavior as an extension of bad manners*
>
> *Manners in terms of the practical vs the traditional*
>
> *Red-ant bites while standing unknowingly on an anthill and conversing with a mule*
>
> *A sign in Tucson for a cosmetic-surgery business called Envy*
>
> *Origin of "on a lighter note"*

What is <u>mande</u>?

Never call upon violence unless put upon by violence, and then repay it threefold

Is it in the nature of time or in how we perceive its passing that we wish for it to pass quickly at a beginning and for it to linger at an end?

He repositioned the freezer-frost bag over his shin, caught his tilting granola cup before it spilled, and continued.

I have held a clear, singular goal for so many years: to carve out of a wilderness setting a beautiful habitation for two. But now? What an unfamiliar feeling to fix my gaze merely on the next town, the next climb, the next possible possibility. Vague, ambiguous, floating, transitory. An indistinguishable horizon. Maybe no horizon. When bicycling across America in '82 I cherished the moment-by-moment existence of a wanderer, but with every pedal stroke I was returning to a place I knew and, I believed, to a purpose from which I needed temporary distance.

But now?

He snapped the retraction mechanism of his pen decisively with his thumb. He pressed the placemarker ribbon into the gutter of his journal, paused, then withdrew it. Again he thumbed the top of his pen, this time slowly until it clicked. Again, he continued.

Is it possible that the girl lied to me? That her father never took her to his bed while her mother hid in the room behind the kitchen? Is it possible that she could feign violent physical spasms and uncontrollable tears when telling a made-up story of abuse that she said began so early in her life she could only describe its chronology as, "I can't remember when it didn't happen"? So much of what she said in that terrible outpouring connected so plainly with the inexplicable events and clues from when she was eight, ten, twelve. Could she have fabricated over the course of so many years the most horrible story imaginable?

She was afraid no one would believe her, that I wouldn't believe her. She reminded me of when she told me something "bad" about her parents and I said that they loved her and wanted what was best for her. She told me her parents were experts at preserving appearances and that people would accept their lies before believing her truth.

I told her I believed her, and that what hadn't made sense years ago finally made sense.

All I can do now is hope that the system she was asked to trust doesn't fail her, that she is happy and prospering in foster care, that she has the help she needs, that her sister and brother can emerge from this ordeal relatively whole.

And . . . I can write the story. I can transcribe letters, texts, voicemails, witness statements, and notes into a volume that tells the truth about a brave girl who was right to trust her own judgment and ask for help. If I cannot use her name I will substitute the one she told me she chose for herself when she was little, when she was wishing she was someone else.

Today she turns seventeen. Happy birthday, Daisy June.

He closed his journal over the ribbon and reached for his computer case. He unzipped the padded bag and opened the machine and pressed the power button, then searched his files. Silently he reread a paragraph that had at once gladdened his heart and troubled his mind.

> I have these entries in my diary from when I was nine and ten where I made up stories about you being my dad. I imagined my life living up on the mountain with you. I can't deny that I still imagine those same things. It's true that I have spent so much of my life

wishing that you were my dad. You are in every way the best possible father I could ever imagine for myself. I know that you are not my dad, but this is just the way I felt/feel. This is very, very personal and hard for me to tell you and I don't expect you to say anything back. I just want you to know.

He returned his computer to its case, pushed the watery plastic bag off of his shin, and dispensed granola from his mug into his left palm. He glanced at Rocinante resting against the wall under a broad barred window, finding himself surprised to see both tires still full of air.

NEARBY *TIENDAS* SOLD ONLY SUGARY DRINKS and packaged snacks; an actual grocery store, the Súper San Francisco Tulum, was a puddled kilometer walk each way. By the time he returned to the hotel he had to climb the rain-slick stairs to his room in half steps, leading with his right leg and following with his left. He could neither point nor contract his foot without pain streaking almost to his knee. He organized his groceries, paid for another night, and collected the morrow's *desayuno pequeño gratis*. He changed into dry clothes and studied his map: four days to Chetumal, he figured, plus a short day into Belize. He supped on tinned pasta with fresh avocado and carrots, and tucked in early to watch *The Great Waldo Pepper* on his ten-inch screen.

Thirteen

He was looking for Muyil and beginning to think he had missed it. The story he read online gave the location of the minor archaeological site as nine point three miles south of Tulum, now three kilometers back.

Nine point three times point six one? He was sure the distance had been specified in miles, not kilometers.

Traffic on the 307 south of Tulum was more sparse than it had been to the north. For the first few kilometers, when there remained a trace of semi-coolness to be enjoyed, a fantasia of black-fringed blue butterflies filled the air above the road like animated giant confetti. A spotty lazuline tapestry, intermittently tufted and stamped, ornamented the pavement. Before his legs were ready he outdistanced a pair of dogs: one quit almost immediately, the other tirelessly kept close for three or four hundred meters.

His shin was snugly bandaged over a compression sock. There was no swelling or discoloration, only stiffness and pain and, as far as he could tell, no reason for either. The supportive pressure was a comfort but served mostly as a reminder to experiment with pedaling technique. He tried rotations with his foot pointed, then locked at ninety degrees, then halfway between. He tried partial push-pull circles around his ankle, then full circles. He tried pedaling at a hundred percent with his right leg and varying degrees less with his left. He pedaled for ten minutes with only his right foot clipped in. He pedaled angrily for five with his right foot free.

"That didn't help," he said to the pain.

Perhaps he had missed Muyil while focused on pedaling, or while laughing at nine-year-old Ramses Emerson's editing of his father's *History of Ancient Egypt* manuscript. He paused the audiobook and positioned his earphone frame to hang behind his neck. He coasted to a stop alongside a guardrail and dismounted.

"Son of a –" he hissed the instant he put weight onto the ball of his left foot. He gripped his handlebar stem and saddle and pushed Rocinante to a patch of partial shade, then sat against the guardrail with one leg outstretched and tipped back the first of his water bottles. Circling overhead was a flock of about thirty vultures.

Although the sun had barely topped the roadside trees, already it was a scorching day. He laughed. He slipped his sunglasses off and hung them from the neck of his shirt and unbuckled his helmet and hooked it over a brake lever. He took another drink.

Am I actually contemplating life between the Tropics of Cancer and Capricorn? he wondered. He tipped his bottle back again and squeezed the last drops out as a mist.

"Not anywhere near Cancún," he assured the vultures.

The city was what the Mexican government intended it to be when transforming a Mayan fishing village into "Gringolandia." Every night from the dock on the lagoon behind his hotel he heard the thump of disco base riding the waves from the Zona Hotelera. He walked six miles one evening to inspect the tourist strip and returned only mentally weary. On his last day there he hired a taxi to bring him to a package-shipping center. Coming back to his hotel the cabby offered to take him to an establishment where, he attested enthusiastically, "you can discharge your *pistola*."

"How can you be in Cancún and not party?" the man queried with considerable animation. "You're alone? I can get you beautiful girls. Very beautiful. From Brazil and Colombia." The man positioned cupped hands in front of his chest to augment his definition of beauty. "They would really like you, I can tell. If you need to go out – and you should, my friend, you should – I take you. What kind of music you like?"

"Keep your hands on the wheel," Renati said. Then he asked, "What does *malecón* mean?"

The driver's eyes opened wide. "You don't like girls?" he

demanded. Renati wished he had brought a book and sat in the back.

"Queer," the cabby exclaimed. "That means *queer*!"

Renati pointed through his window at a sign in a shopping center and read, "Banamex Malecón Americas."

"*Qué?* Oh! Ocean view. You said *maricón*!"

When they stopped in the hotel parking lot the driver offered a business card and said, "My number is on the back. If you need to discharge your *pistola*, you call me!"

HE PASSED THE SIGN FOR MUYIL a few kilometers later. He checked his rear-view mirror and circled back and walked Rocinante to the admission kiosk. He had hoped to enter with his bicycle, but the attendant assured him it would be safe parked against the wall of the *baño* building. He did not try to explain that he wanted the bicycle for support, and as he left it behind to begin his solo tour he wondered if he also wanted it for company.

He had since he was young been attracted to abandoned habitations. America's western ghost towns were his favorite, but cellar holes in New England, forgotten farmhouses on the plains, and adobe ruins in the desert all gave him a similar feeling, which he could not quite describe.

Did it come from curiosity about the lives of those who once gave life to a place? Or from an interest in days-gone-by architecture and construction in a vanished, unrepeatable time? Was it attraction to a quiet that seemed deeper than other kinds of quiet?

He realized, as he gazed through a smoke-blackened doorway into a sunless Mayan room, that almost every one of his past occupations offered moments, *cherished* moments, of solitude and quiet: locking the doors and counting the till at two in the morning at the Phoenix nightclub; servicing a pickup truck on a Sunday afternoon in the Little Rock auto-repair shop; training when the ski hill was closed or in the dark or in a snowstorm; working the graveyard shift as a security guard in an echoey Manchester warehouse; deadheading a Trailways motorcoach from Boston back to the garage; hiking home to a ghost-town cabin through a mile of dusky forest after a day of timber falling; gazing across rows of empty seats at a darkened stage in an empty theater.

He limped alone through the ruins along a leaf-sprinkled path bordered by ancient mossy stone under a verdant canopy. He remembered his camera and took a few pictures and returned to Rocinante, doing his best to put only left-side weight on his heel.

He decided he would one day identify the various kinds of quiet, beginning with the quiet of a place barren of its former creative life.

HE REACHED UNDER HIS HANDLEBAR and pushed a button and said, "Start. Many of the houses – huts and shacks, really – along this excellent modern highway appear to have no water. The evolution of our species clearly still exists in its earlier stages. Does technological advancement impose a threat to the tranquility of humans further down the developmental ladder? *Threat* is not the right word...."

He paused. He drank from his second bottle, then continued.

"Perhaps a culture not yet capable of creating new gadgets is also not prepared for adding them to life. The trickle-down effect of this, while beneficial in many ways, presents hazards when made cheaply available to those who cannot understand them, never mind create them. *Hazard* isn't the right word, either. End."

He increased his speed up a gentle incline. A juvenile brown basilisk streaked across both lanes.

Fourteen

When the receptionist at his Felipe Carrillo Puerto hotel asked, *"Cuántas noches?"* he answered, *"Uno,"* but after what should have been an easy short walk to the Super Chedraui became a pain-aggravating hour down wrong streets carrying gallon jugs of water and a straining pair of plastic grocery bags, he requested two more nights with meals in his room. He ventured out only when he needed the lobby's Wi-Fi to study lower-leg anatomy and to send the emails he composed with a word-processing program. His shin became increasingly tender and tight with inactivity. Stretching, massage, warm-water soaks in his room's plastic trash can, and towel-wrapped ice from the hotel kitchen were of little help. He knew he could either rest until the injury healed or push and make it worse. He needed to give it a week, but not in Felipe Carrillo Puerto, Bacalar, or Chetumal.

Not in a city.

He knew nothing about Mahahual except that it would require a round-trip detour, and he knew that a hundred and thirty kilometers on an injured leg with heavy rain in the forecast was maybe not a good idea, but the pictures he saw of the Costa Maya beach inspired him to book a seven-day hotel reservation. He emailed the manager to say he was arriving by bicycle and that it would probably be late in the day. He lay awake a long time that night, excited about his plan, and woke early after barely five hours of sleep.

HE BEGAN WITH BOND'S vigorous interpretation of Astor Piazzolla's "Libertango" and Santana's "Smooth." He misread a street sign and turned west on 184 instead of east to 307, which looked more like a side street than a main road. It felt wrong within a few minutes but under the heavy clouds there were no direction-orienting shadows and he was unsure of his error until he passed the Super Chedraui.

"Good job," he said to Rocinante.

He offered *buenas dios* to a young couple with a baby on a tiny motorbike, to a skinny dog, to a taxi driver who yielded to him on a side street, to a wrinkled man on a wobbly-wheeled antique tricycle, to a middle-aged man on a shiny new tricycle laden with snacks for sale, to a motley pair of cows standing in the bed of a pickup truck, to a darkening sky that suggested rain within the hour. He swerved to avoid crushing the world's largest millipede, then U-turned for a closer look. He wished he had seen an armadillo in Texas.

The highway south of Felipe Carrillo Puerto was straight and nearly flat, bisecting luxuriant greenery, finally devoid of the trash-fire smoke that had assaulted his lungs since Cancún. He pedaled hard for twenty-seven kilometers to a preprogrammed soundtrack of fast-tempo music – normally not what he would choose for morning listening – and he had just begun looking for a place to rest when an admonishing raindrop splashed the right lens of his sunglasses. He knew he should have installed his pannier covers before leaving the hotel.

He braked beneath a tree overhanging the road on the northbound side and was drenched before he had the first bag covered.

*Not that it makes any difference with this humidit*y, he thought.

He zipped neoprene covers over his shoes and transferred his music player from his shirt pocket to his handlebar bag and squeezed water from the padded leather palms of his gloves. He crossed the road and, despite the crowned pavement, felt resistance and left a wake. He mounted and found his cadence with his head down and rain streaming in a little waterfall from the visor of his helmet. A tractor-trailer passed straddling the painted broken line, the wave that struck his left side nearly propelled him into the grass.

Judy Collins sang, unperturbed, exquisitely, of a blizzard in Colorado. She was right, he thought, about how one can talk to a stranger. It was how one should talk to any person worth the time of a conversation.

It rained hard for thirty minutes, subsided for twenty, then drizzled steadily for an hour. He had gone another forty kilometers when the sun broke through the clouds and steam began rising from the pavement.

Halfway to Mahahual and his leg felt great, he told himself.

He lunched on *sardinas*, avocado, flour tortillas, and dried apricots under the roof of a green cage of a bus stop. He longed for cold chocolate milk; he settled for warm *agua pura*. His bar bag and pantry bag were dry, but his panniers were wet on the bottom where rain had pooled under the covers. Apparently their water-resistant coating resisted water in both directions.

The sky turned dark again and he sat through another downpour. No buses stopped, but a dented Ford Maverick with a badly cracked – *was that duct tape?* – windshield pulled into the bus lane and idled noisily for the duration. He noticed when it drove away that the rear window was part plywood, part green trash bag, seamed with wrinkled silver tape. He heard his telephone ring faintly, as if from an alternate time, then beep.

He didn't realize it worked in Mexico. He was only carrying it for the camera and alarm.

It should be forty-five minutes more to the coastal turnoff, he thought, then fifty kilometers – maybe two and a half hours counting a sandwich break – to Mahahual. Arrival by five-thirty, he estimated.

The clouds appeared to be thinning. He hoped Hotel Luna de Plata's restaurant served spaghetti.

THE SUN EMERGED just as he spotted the sign for the Mahahual road, and he boosted Dire Straits' "Sultans of Swing" and pedaled as fast as he could to the junction and leaned with a flourish into the turn. He downshifted twice in the first hundred meters and rode two or three hundred more before realizing he was pushing a headwind.

"Okay!" he shouted into the minor gale. "There's an ocean

beach at the end of this road and I'm going to make use of it!"

He reversed direction and adjusted his speed until he felt no wind at his back or in his face. Eighteen ... nineteen ... twenty ... He swerved again into the resistance and yelled, "Is that it? Twenty kilometers per?"

He advanced his music player through a lineup of soft rock and stopped when he reached Gordon Lightfoot's "Wreck of the Edmund Fitzgerald." He had considered changing his name to that of the capsized freighter, but decided self-mockingly it might be bad luck.

He needed a break after barely forty minutes. He leaned Rocinante against his parking stand and made a peanut-butter-and-honey tortilla roll while sitting on the concrete base of a high-voltage transmission tower. He ate his snack and emptied water-bottle five, then walked back to the road. His legs were dotted with blood-engorged mosquitoes. He brushed them away and glowered at the brown smears and red streaks. For the first time since he had left that morning he felt tired.

Tired, dirty, and, he admitted, very sore.

"Okay," he said quietly to the wind, wiping his legs clean with a handful of damp grass. According to his map he had gone two thirds the distance to the only bend in the road. After the bend, he calculated, it would be thirty-six kilometers to the end of the road – which somehow totaled five kilometers more than his original figuring. He would arrive before sundown, at least, although he wasn't sure where the hotel was located since the online map showed it in the middle of an empty dead-end boulevard by a long dock.

HE STOOD BENEATH the Mahahual lighthouse facing the setting sun. The wind in his face felt so much better here than it had felt fifty kilometers back. He was certain that if he were to recline on the concrete he would sleep soundly until morning. He photographed the lighthouse and the post-card-perfect coastal vista, and pointed Rocinante in the direction described to him in English by two men ambling home from work.

"Go down the road, not too far, and go left. Left?" "No, right," said the other man. "Right. Left. Go until you see the hotel. What name?" "Ko'ox Matan Ka'an?" "Right." "Take a left at that hotel." "And then a right." "And then you will see your hotel."

He rode west a ways and took a left and a left and a right and pedaled slowly for what he was sure was too far. He turned back along a foot-traffic-only road and found a sign with a map of the town and saw that he hadn't gone far enough. The sun was down and Nat King Cole was crooning "Non Dimenticar" when he dismounted a few minutes later in front of Hotel Luna de Plata. It was as becoming in person as it had been in pictures.

He drained water-bottle seven and pushed Rocinante unsteadily through deep sand to the glass-fronted thatch-roof building. A lithe woman of about thirty – Hispanic or Lebanese, he thought – approached him. She wore a white cotton blouse with blue jeans and canvas sneakers. Her black hair was swept in a heavy gleaming tumble over her left shoulder.

"*Hola, buenos noches*," she said in a low-toned voice. "Are you okay?"

He tugged his headset from his ears. He wondered if she was a guest or an employee. He answered, "Yes. I have a reservation."

"I know." Her full lips pursed slightly when she smiled. "I was coming back from Mexico City when I read your email. The owner doesn't speak very good English. But you found the hotel."

She held a room key between long light-brown fingers.

He lifted his rig onto a sand-dusted terrace and followed her through a breezeway that opened onto a tropical courtyard. She wore an airy floral perfume. Or, he thought, perhaps it was shampoo. She stopped in front of a railed-in porch and turned to face him. She said, "I thought you would want to be on the ground floor, but there's a TV in the upstairs room."

He shook his head. "No. No television."

A salmon cloud in the darkening sky gave the courtyard a dreamlike radiance. The zephyr that swayed the palms cooled his still-damp skin and stirred her hair. He added, "I apologize for . . . . Well, I'm sure I don't –"

Her eyes met his and she said quietly, "You smell like rain."

"I do?" It wasn't what he meant to say.

"Are you hungry?"

"Do you have spaghetti?" wasn't what he meant to say either.

She smiled and took a half step toward him and pressed the room key into his palm. She replied, "Carbonara?" and told him her name.

IN THE MORNING, seated in the far corner of the hotel dining room at a table of Tzalam wood, he gazed through a salt-air-tarnished screen past brown-painted beach furniture at blue-green waves breaking white over the barrier reef. He asked of the waves the question he sometimes asked of a landscape when holding open the flaps of his tent at sunrise.

"Could this be home?"

Fifteen

Mahahual, he knew, would be hard to leave. His room was comfortable, meals in the hotel restaurant were delicious and often private, the village was nearly devoid of tourists except for two occasions when cruise ships docked for a brief visit, and the constant coastal breeze made the summer heat tolerable. On the afternoon of his second day he had waded in the shallows of the Mesoamerican Barrier Reef with his black camp pants rolled above his calves. At breakfast the following morning the hotel manager handed him bathing trunks in a shopping bag and, smiling her pretty pursed-lip smile, said, "Better than long pants for swimming."

He wrote for an hour on his porch every morning, stretched and exercised his injury in the warm Gulf almost every afternoon, wrote for an hour in the dark on the beach almost every night, finished reading Franklin's autobiography, and occasionally watched movies in bed over a sporadic community Internet signal. The setting was serene, picturesque, romantic, interesting, calming and stimulating in nearly equal parts, and tempting.

He departed for Bacalar on the nineteenth day, an hour after sunrise. It had taken a week before he could walk without favoring his leg. He tried a ten-kilometer test ride on the ninth day and, sprinting to avoid four sets of snapping dog jaws, lost one or two days' healing. He rode again on day thirteen and felt minor pain, but by day seventeen there was only a slight stiffness.

He had anticipated sorrow when leaving Mahahual; he had not anticipated a headwind. Why, he wondered, after weeks of unremitting coastal easterlies, was there now a twenty-kilometer wind out of the west? Within an hour he encountered a second minor annoyance: the smooth asphalt he had failed to appreciate on his way in had since been top-coated with an aggressively pebbled surface that buzzed under his Schwalbes.

Head down. Music up. *The Seduction of Claude Debussy* did wonders to overcome resistance to forward motion. He turned south onto Mexico 307 just before noon.

WEST OF PEDRO ANTONIO SANTOS he remembered that his cell phone had rung almost three weeks ago. He stopped at a Pemex station and bought a chocolate milk and sat on a dusty curb and opened his phone. He switched it on, found that he had a signal, and pressed *one* for voicemail.

"This is Doug Pfeiffer," said the recording. "I'm trying to reach the Nijinsky of skiing. I was wondering if he would mind if I nominate him for the Skiing Hall of Fame. I hope he gets this message."

He pressed *end* and closed his phone. He finished his milk and continued south. He would email Mr. Pfeiffer and tell him he didn't mind, although in truth he didn't mind either way. He could still feel that first love of his life in his sinews and in his soul, and even like he could return to it if he desired.

A tendon above his left ankle seemed to be catching on the upstroke. Perhaps, he thought, a hundred-plus kilometers was overly ambitious after recovering from an injury. Then again, with only thirty-seven to go riding a perfect expedition bicycle over level ground in a light tailwind through sun-varnished greenery after nineteen days and nights on an unpopulated tropical beach – so what! He laughed and found an easy cadence and rode an extra five exploratory kilometers after arriving in Bacalar, one of Mexico's eighty-three "Pueblo Mágico."

THERE WAS NOTHING he could find about Bacalar that was magical. On the contrary, the town was ugly and unpleasant. His mid-level hotel room was dark, damp, and dreary – although the chirping gecko on the wall outside his door seemed cheerful enough. The included breakfast of toasted white bread and watery coffee was made comical by a plump aproned woman pushing a dust mop in circles around the dining room while humming a Barry White tune. The streets and businesses were drab and untidy. Perhaps, he thought, after Mahahual's lightness and charm it was just the contrast, but he was glad to leave Bacalar and he did so at full speed in an early-morning drizzle.

At a convenience store two hours later he waited in the checkout line behind three black-helmeted, ballistic-vested Policía Federal. When he reached the counter and paid for his orange juice, he turned to see the officers gathered around his bicycle where it leaned beneath the big storefront window, pointing at and discussing the item secured by a quick-release strap to the top of his right-rear pannier.

"Oops," he said to himself. He moved to where he could stand under an air-conditioning vent and opened his juice and took a sip, watching. He had designed two separate camp tools – a narrow knife-edged shovel and a reconfigured geologist's hammer – that could be assembled together in seconds to form a third tool with an entirely different function. The two-foot-long instrument was inconspicuous over a black pannier, but against a yellow rain cover it became glaringly obvious.

The Federales spent several minutes in conversation while variously nodding and shrugging and shaking their heads. Then, as if having reached agreement, they crossed the small parking lot to where their blue-and-white Ford pickup and three other officers waited. One got into the passenger seat and two took their places standing behind the cab, and the truck sped away.

Renati exited the store and removed and stowed five of his six bag covers, leaving, as always, the left-rear pannier dressed for visibility. He pedaled back to the main road, hoping that the *policía* had concluded that MICA – his Multipurpose Indestructible Cyclist Accessory – was no more illegal to carry in Mexico than the machetes he had in mind when fabricating it.

IT WAS LATE MORNING when he arrived in Chetumal. He stopped at a bank to exchange Mexican pesos for Belizean dollars and was told they had none, then checked into a hotel a block from the bay and showered and changed and walked to Museum de la Cultura Maya. He returned just after five and walked for another twenty minutes along the low wall separating Chetumal Bay's gentle green swells from Boulevard Bahia.

He had expected by now to be in Honduras or Guatemala, but he didn't mind the delay. He was not in a hurry and he had wasted no time – an expense he loathed and for which he seldom budgeted. Days, he bemoaned, were usually several hours too short, and, to make the deficit even more exasperating, a week needed at least eight of them. An additional September or October would comfortably compliment a thirteen-month year, he reckoned, but how the calendar was rearranged didn't matter so long as he could perpetually accomplish "just one more" of whatever task he was attempting before the interruption of sleep or a meal or a scheduled commitment.

Or death, he added to the list without levity.

HE HAD MEANT TO REST only a few minutes but the room was dark, the bed was comfortable, and Frank Muller's sonorous narration of *Red Square* was inexorably soothing. It was eight fifty-five when he emerged from a wake-up shower to dress and hurry downstairs for super in the hotel restaurant.

His waitress was apologetic while informing him that the kitchen had closed eight minutes earlier and that they did not have English muffins, which he had done his best to describe. When she returned with his order of coffee and *bolillo* she asked, "*Eres el hombre de la bicicleta?*"

He answered, "*Sí. Soy el hombre de la bicicleta,*" and brushed a tracing of instant-coffee dust from the rim of his cup.

She asked, "*Por qué estás montando tu bicicleta hasta ahora? Por qué no montas en el autobús?*"

He split one of the two small loaves and asked the girl for butter. When she returned he replied, "Because bridges freeze first and there are too many gravels and too few beacons."

"*Qué?*" she asked, laughing lightly. Set off by olive skin and burgundy lipstick, her smile was dazzling. She looked to be between sixteen and eighteen. "*No hay puentes congelados en México!*"

He nodded. "*Mi español no es muy bueno.* Do you know the 'Roadrunner' cartoon?"

Her smile broadened. "*Y el coyote? Me encanta esa caricatura!*"

He smiled back at her and said, "Just runnin' down the road decides he's havin' fun."

She laughed again, then paused and frowned and looked puzzled. Fifteen minutes later she met him at the cash register. She asked if he had American dollars. He unzipped his wallet and opened the compartment that held his passport. He had a twenty and two singles. She raised an index finger, walked a zigzag path through the empty dining room to his table, and came back holding the twin twenty-peso notes he had left as a tip.

"*Puedo tener dólares?*" she asked quietly. She extended her hand and added, "For one dollars?"

He withdrew the singles and pressed them over the smaller blue notes on her palm. She shook her head and placed the pesos on the counter behind him and said with unusual earnestness, "*Gracias.*"

He unzipped his wallet's coin compartment and sorted through change while she watched. He found a dime and a nickel.

"Heads or tails?" he asked.

"*Qué?*"

He indicated Jefferson's silvery likeness and said, "Heads." He turned the coin over and pointed and said, "Tails."

She frowned slightly and said, "Heads?"

He flipped the nickel with his thumb, caught it on his right palm, and slapped it onto the back of his left hand. He uncovered it. He showed her and said, "Heads."

He gave her the coin. She smiled and nodded. He sent the dime spinning into the air, caught it on his right palm, and slapped it onto the back of his left hand.

"Heads!" she claimed enthusiastically.

He peered secretively into the shadow between his hands. The girl watched closely, her eyes lustrous with anticipation. He shook his head in mock disappointment and added the dime to the small account on her palm, then closed her fingers around it.

He paid his bill and returned by the light of streetlamps to the seawall to sit facing the bay with his legs suspended over smooth wave-splashed stones. He could just make out a few stars beyond the city's glow. To the waves and the stars and to shores he could not see he said, "'Twas brillig, and the slithy toves did gyre and gimble in the wabe: All mimsy were the borogoves, and the mome raths outgrabe."

He wondered why she had remained in Wyoming. Why she had not started her new life as a single woman somewhere sunny, sandy, warm. Cabo San Lucas or Punta Mita. Or at least southern California. Had her oft-expressed preference for a summer-dress climate been something else he misinterpreted?

He reached back and down to the base of the wall and trailed his fingers along the ground in search of a stone or a stick, for something to throw into the water. He found tufts of coarse grass between gritty concrete slabs. He found a plastic straw. He felt a droplet of rain on his forehead, then another on his arm and another on his neck. He stood on the wall and pushed his hands into his pockets and peered into the darkness toward where he imagined Sarteneja to be. He noticed that he was within a few feet of a canon barrel bedded into the wall and aimed fixedly over the bay at . . . what?

Tomorrow he would cross into Belize.

Finally! he thought, although he did not know why Belize seemed a worthy goal. More heat. More humidity. He would coast into Corozal well before sundown and stand gazing back across the water toward where he had been standing tonight. Which would by then be yesterday.

To Yesterday he whispered, "We help the season at Gruxley Allen Pie Pie call the meow meow," and in the company of Alonso Quijano, Arkady Renko, and Clayton Buell, he meandered north in the rain on Boulevard Bahia until he was soaked to the skin and chilled to the bone.

Sixteen

"Purposeofvisit?" The blue-uniformed Belize customs official slurred the words together. She didn't bother to look up from Renati's passport.

"Jussridinthrough," he answered. The woman raised her eyes, but not her head.

"What?" she asked.

"Good morning," he suggested. "Welcome to Belize."

She displayed a bored scowl and repeated, "Purposeofvisit?"

Crossing into Belize felt to Renati like a landmark event, almost like an opportunity. He was curious about, and in some ways attracted to, this English-speaking Massachusetts-size nation shoehorned between Mexico, Central America, and the Caribbean. He had heard good stories about the people, the land, and the banks; and bad stories about the roads, violent crime, and political corruption. Although he was not merely journeying through en route to Guatemala or Honduras, he had no particular plan beyond signing a document in San Pedro and touring the Belize Zoo. He did not consider himself a vacationer, but neither was he planning to relocate to the mountain jungles of the Cayo District. At least, he affirmed, not yet.

Purpose of visit?

He glanced at his uncommonly beautiful expedition bicycle standing against the slate-blue block wall eight feet away. Who, he wanted to know, could gaze upon Rocinante and not understand?

Crocodile Dundee suddenly popped into his mind and proposed helpfully, "Tell her you're on a rideabout."

He pointed to his bicycle and said, "Belize is between Mexico and where I'm going on that." Seeing her unchanged countenance he added, "Tourism."

His panniers were searched with the same lack of interest, and fifteen minutes later he was walking his bicycle along a tall chain-link fence over powdery gravel toward pavement he hoped was the road to Corozal. He paused in a shady spot for a drink of water and an avocado while reassembling MICA from border-crossing configuration to travel configuration. He rinsed the blade of his jackknife and dried it on a square of paper napkin, tossed the avocado pit and skin under a tree, attached his left foot to the pedal, and was at last bicycling in Belize.

Why am I so happy to be here? he wondered.

"It's too hot and humid to be happy," he replied into the sweltering crosswind. But he knew the answer. Belize was a new place, somewhere he had never been. It was a first and felt like a first, and he needed a first.

He stopped to rest in the shade of a squat barn a hundred yards – imperial units, he reminded himself, now that he was in the former British Honduras – east of the Northern Highway. The partly cloudy sky was filled with innumerable soaring, circling crows. While striding through long grass toward the structure he flushed ten or twelve of the silent big birds – vultures, he realized, not crows – and watched them climb to join their speck-small brethren. It was barely twelve thirty and he was down three bottles of water. He drank a fourth with a pair of drippy peanut-butter-and-honey corn-tortilla flats. He snapped a picture of the hovering winged dots and left a small pile of crumbly tortilla pieces on the top of a fence post, then returned to the highway.

As soon as he reached cruising speed on the low-grade asphalt he placed his right hand affectionately on Rocinante's sea-foam-green top tube and asked, "How could anyone not be in awe of you?"

HE BOUGHT ORANGE JUICE at a Chinese grocery store and waited in line at a bank for Belizean dollars while monitoring his bicycle through a plate-glass window. Since there was no one at the Sea Breeze Hotel when he arrived, he pedaled Corozal's streets for an hour to the music of Pablo Cruise and Michael Crawford. It was just after three thirty when he returned to the hotel and met the owner – a plucky Brit whose candid replies to whining online reviews caused Renati to want to support his business – and paid for a two-night stay. He carried his bags and bicycle in three trips up the blue concrete stairs to his room, stepping each time over a gray three-legged dog. He showered and changed and, accepting the invitation of a pair of children playing on the hotel's white-painted dock, stepped out of his sneakers and socks and into the warm green water.

It was sundown when he walked to RD's Diner for an excellent Creole dinner, and dark when he bought a chocolate bar and a banana from a grocery stand while following Fifth Street to a bay-side park a few blocks northeast of his hotel. He chose a bench away from the street lights and sat to enjoy his dessert in the upper-seventies breeze. A young mother pushed a little girl in a swing suspended by chains from not-very-straight multicolored logs; three men talked quietly around a table under a spindly gazebo's thatch roof.

It was strange, he thought, to hear conversational English in a place that felt so foreign.

After a while he stood and found a garbage bin for his candy wrapper and banana peel and crossed the sparse grass to the seawall and sat with his back against a painted stone buttress. There were no lights on the water and no stars to be seen. The gazebo trio had wandered off. Lapping waves and the occasional squeak of swinging swing chains were the only sounds to be heard.

A few drops of rain fell and a scattering of stars appeared to the northeast, over the Costa Maya. He thought about friends from his past and about what had made them friends. He thought about his parents and how close he had been to them until a familial rift twenty-four years ago, the last time they would see each other. He thought about his brother and their recent reconciliation. He brought clearly to mind teachers from high school and found it curious that he could remember none from college. He evoked lovers and jobs and places he had lived and sights he had seen and imagined all of it – the people, the work, the locales –

accompanying him on his ride.

Miles and years have at least one attribute in common, he thought: both seem to pass slowly at first, until suddenly there are many behind and not so many ahead.

He recalled a sunny winter morning, sitting with Ragnar on the mammoth flat boulders that formed the steps to his cabin. He had asked aloud, "Who am I?" and, setting his coffee mug aside, composed with a carpenter's pencil his answer on the back of a list of chores. Ragnar, looking especially debonair in his red-and-blue fleece sweater, had simply lifted his head from crossed paws and offered a look that said, "You're Mike."

Ragnar was the only person allowed to call him that.

A couple motored by on a tiny scooter. Renati was alone in the park. He pressed the knurled crown on his watch and the face glowed blue: it was ten forty, twenty minutes to lockup at the Sea Breeze.

He rose to stand on the wall and gaze across the black expanse to where he had stood the night before, but his mind was on what lay ahead. He knew, despite his need to be a stranger in a strange land, that he was not at heart a nomad.

Seventeen

The woman who opened the screen door at the top of the hotel stairs asked, "Do you know where I can find the manager? I think he is called Gwyn."

Renati stood in blazing sun on the little roof deck outside his room, shirtless and dripping with sweat, a bicycle wheel braced between bare knees and a compact pump gripped in both hands. He gave the pump seven more strokes and paused in his count at two hundred.

"No," he answered. "But yesterday he was here around three thirty."

She was in her mid-twenties, about five-five dressed in an off-white cotton blouse and khaki shorts and leather sandals. Her brown hair was gathered in a loose bun. She was slim and pretty and as French in appearance as her accent suggested.

"Are you staying here?" he asked.

"I hope so," she replied, smiling. "I'll come back later."

He watched her pause to step over the dog on the stairs. He hoped so, too.

SHE WAS IN THE LOBBY, kneeling on the teal-and-rust-red tiles stroking the head of Gwyn's other pup, a brown four-legged shorthair, when he descended the stairs on his way to supper.

She looked up at him over her shoulder and asked, "Do you know a good place to eat?"

"I do," he replied. "Would you like to walk there with me?"

Her name was Abelle. She was a fashion-industry professional from Paris who had, on what sounded to Renati like a whim, flown to Cancún and taken an apartment while searching for summer employment. She had boarded a bus to Corozal and would stay the night before traveling on to Sarteneja across the bay. She spoke French, English, Spanish, Portuguese, and Russian. She wanted a baby someday but not a husband. She was twenty-five years old.

They strolled slowly back from RD's by way of the park. They sat on the Sea Breeze dock for an hour and then on the lobby sofa, talking until after one o'clock. She sat close to him, or he to her, and he found their occasional contact stirring. They met five hours later at the foot of the stairs and he walked her to the municipal dock to catch the morning ferry to Sarteneja. She gave him her Cancún phone number and kissed him on the cheek and said maybe she would see him in Orange Walk.

He returned to the hotel eating the pastry she had offered from a paper bag in her knapsack. He didn't know if his phone would work in Belize, but he doubted he would see her again.

HE STAYED TWO MORE DAYS in Corozal. He and another guest, a bartender from Chicago, hired Gwyn to boat them across the bay to see the Cerros Mayan site – which they only discerned from a distance while skimming the waves en route to a resort of the same name.

"What's your attitude on bribes?" the resort's American owner asked him over a lunch of *ceviche de pescado*.

The question arose from an exchange of tales of Belizean police taking payments to ignore various legal infractions.

"My attitude?" Renati asked. "I don't know about attitude, but my answer would be *no*."

"Well, you should think of it as tipping," his host suggested constructively.

He departed for Orange Walk mid-morning the next day after a brief photo session in front of the hotel.

And what a day it will be! he thought. A relaxing thirty-two miles of level pedaling with a mild tailwind in a new country. He had not yet decided whether he would take the Lamanai Mayan

City tour by boat up the New River or continue the next day to Belize City, and it did not matter. His music would be the intonations of a rural-Belize Saturday; his pace would be whatever his legs felt like producing.

He stopped for a cup of yogurt where the road out of Corozal joined the Northern Highway and discovered that his indispensable folding bicycle stand was missing. He knew immediately what had happened: after sliding it temporarily under his pantry-bag webbing so that Gwyn could take farewell photographs, he had neglected to secure it where it belonged. He checked his odometer: he had come ten point one miles.

He laid Rocinante in the long roadside grass and sipped his yogurt. He considered calling Gwyn and asking him to search in front of the hotel, but he wasn't sure he had the number or, still, if his phone would work. He pulled it from his handlebar bag and pressed the power button.

Thirty seconds later it chirped loudly and he nearly dropped it in surprise. He viewed the display. It read, *Hola, Michael. I'll be in Orange Walk tonight. Will you be there?*

He looked at his watch and replied, *Hola, Abelle. I am riding south now but lost something on the road. I should arrive in Orange Walk by four.*

He walked Rocinante in a U-turn, mounted and pedaled a few hundred yards, then, braking to a stop and straddling his top tube, selected ELO's "Telephone Line" on his music player and began backtracking into what had before been a pleasant tailwind. Nine miles toward Corozal he spotted his stand undamaged at the edge of the pavement in the opposite lane. He restored it to its rightful place, drank some water, and checked his phone.

Where are you staying? queried a new text message.

He keyed *Hotel de la Fuente* and closed his phone and started south under an ill-tempered sky. Where his planned paved route turned west to connect with the Northern Highway he continued straight over a hard-packed chalky road through Libertad.

"Whenever possible," he advised Rocinante, "make the most of an unexpected delay or detour. Make it a new opportunity, and intentional."

FROM HIS SEAT ON A GRASSY BANK in the shade of an umbrella-like feathery-leafed tree, he admired his bicycle against a backdrop of swaying sugarcane. He was traveling a strange road under strange skies between sparsely spaced decrepit residences. A coatimundi, the first he had ever seen, loped silently from the tall grass on his side of the road into the taller cane on the other.

While stowing his lunch leftovers he heard, then saw, a small motorcycle putt-putting toward him ahead of a plume of gray-white dust. The rider stopped, switched off the bike's engine, set his kickstand, and dismounted. He was a chubby man, five-eight, early thirties, wearing a dirty baseball cap and an untucked green-and-brown-striped polo shirt over bagged-out blue jeans. Under the shirt, above his left hip, was the outline of a pistol butt.

Renati loosened the strap over MICA and transferred his sunglasses to his handlebar bag. He raised his right foot to his left knee and snugged the hook-and-loop closures over his shoe, then did the same for the other side.

"Hi," said the man as he approached.

"Hello," Renati answered. He stepped around the back of his bicycle, leaving the fingers of his right hand resting lightly atop his pantry bag, and asked, "What kind of pistol are you carrying?"

The man halted, still a few feet away. He looked startled. Renati could just make out a faded security-company insignia on the front of the ball cap.

"Oh!" said the man as if reminded he was armed. "It's only a twenty-two."

"Smith and Wesson?" Renati asked. "Ruger?"

The man tugged at his shirt hem and exposed the black grip and stainless frame of a Smith 2206 in a cheap nylon belt holster. It looked like it had seen many users.

"May I?" Renati asked extending his left hand.

The man grinned proudly, unholstered the weapon, and offered it muzzle first. Renati took it, half-ejected the magazine, and jacked the slide. The action was dry; the chamber empty. He released the slide, reengaged the magazine, checked the safety, and returned the piece grip first.

"A good pistol," he said.

The man nodded, still grinning. He slid the gun back into its holster and covered it with his shirt. "I'm the security officer for all of these cane farms," he said, indicating with a sweep of his arm the surrounding area. "It's a big job because there are a lot of people who might steal sugar cane. I live about a mile that way." He pointed south. "If you are riding that way you can have lunch with me."

ABELLE WAS WAITING for him on the sidewalk in front of Hotel de la Fuenta. Her pleated green shorts made her tanned legs look thin; her ivory tank-top suggested she wasn't thin all over. Despite having traveled two hours in an unairconditioned bus she looked enchanting, Renati thought, whereas he was a mess. A sweat-streaked gray film coated his legs and forearms. He suspected his face was not much cleaner.

"It's *my* turn to take *you* to dinner, okay?" she asked.

She helped carry his panniers up the stairs and sat on his bed while he showered. She talked to him through the bathroom door while he shaved. She seemed not to mind waiting and content to be there. Over their meal she tried to teach him how to roll his r's. He suggested they quit after he finally managed *Rrrrocinante* three times in a row.

They said goodnight on the sidewalk beside the passenger van that would take her back to Sarteneja. She kissed his cheek and said maybe she would see him in San Pedro. Ten hours later, after a superb breakfast in Hotel de la Fuente's dining room, he departed Orange Walk in a downpour. By the time he found his way through puddle-bestrewn road construction he was generously painted with mud. By the time he reached the junction above Carmelita the unrelenting deluge had washed him clean.

He listened to the first of his Scottish-burred Spanish lessons and practiced rolling his r's.

ALL THAT WAS LACKING was a chorus of angels when the sun pierced the gloom at the district border. Fairy-tale mist levitated above lustrous pavement; a double rainbow materialized over glistening green shrubland to the east. He stopped once for a hurriedly assembled sandwich, then again to photograph an elaborate driveway gate with a bicycle built into it, and then, an hour later, to appreciate a grand view of the tree-lined Belize River. Six miles outside Belize City, in increasingly heavy traffic, a cyclist began drafting him. Renati pulled his left earphone loose and glanced at his cyclometer: sixteen miles per hour. At a wide spot in the road he hugged the shoulder and motioned for the cyclist to pass.

Instead, the rider moved alongside and began a conversation. He was about twenty, slight of build and dark-skinned, in a white-and-black logo-embellished jersey. He rode an older Italian steel-framed bicycle in good condition and spoke with an accent Renati could not place. Maybe Jamaican, he thought, understanding only half of what the young man shouted. After a few minutes Renati told him to take the lead. Within a mile their pace began to slacken.

He did not want to be riding after dark in Belize City. His cyclometer read thirteen miles per hour.

He accelerated past his escort just north of the Haulover Bridge and bade him farewell, pushing, he knew, too hard for the end of a bad-weather fifty-five-mile day, but he had a hotel to find and only a half hour of daylight in which to find it. Two hours later, after three miles of wandering through torn-up lightless streets and after four pedestrians and two homeowners said they knew of no hotel in the area, he coasted to a stop outside an unmarked high-walled property on a corner in a residential neighborhood, one block from the waterfront.

Last chance, he thought, squeezing a last sip from his last water bottle while studying a massive green sheet-metal gate.

Within a minute a dark late-model Toyota Landcruiser paralleled the culvert along the foot of the wall and parked. The driver's-side door opened and out stepped a petite woman with a wavy blonde bob, followed through the same door by a small black-haired boy in a soccer uniform. The woman wore a tailored teal skirt suit and high-heeled shoes. She waved to Renati where he stood straddling his bicycle and exclaimed, "I was wondering if you were going to make it!"

HE WAS THE ONLY GUEST in the facility, which, he surmised, might recently have been a school residence hall. The woman was the building's owner and would be, once the conversion was complete, the hotel manager. Renati paid and signed a rental agreement and was given three keys – one for the gate, one for the front door, one for his room. The wide-awake eight-year-old footballer handed him a huge ripe mango, then trailed his mother out the front door and down the steps and through the steel gate to the sidewalk. Between clean sheets in an air-conditioned characterless concrete enclosure, Renati surrendered easily to dreamless sleep.

Eighteen

He was out of coffee. He had shared the last of the good stuff with the hotel manager in Mahahual, and had since been sipping weak restaurant brew. He was also out of food except for scant scrapings of peanut butter and a not-very-tasty brand of sardines in tomato sauce. In the painted-plywood cupboards of a communal kitchen he found pots and pans, dishes and glassware, plastic storage containers and paper towels. In the refrigerator he found one egg, an open carton of low-fat milk, and a foil pouch of instant coffee.

Under the mango trees beneath the second-story windowed corridor outside his room, big crabs lurked in holes in the sandy soil, cautiously venturing out a few inches, then, with surprising speed, retreating into darkness. Judging by the half-eaten decomposing fruit littering the ground beneath the trees, the creatures' choice of domicile was a good one.

Renati sat on the narrow window ledge watching the crabs and sipping his coffee-like beverage. He turned the latch of the casement pane beside him and pushed the glass outward, then pulled it back and closed the latch.

It was like opening an oven door.

He remembered the breakfast-size mango the boy had given him, and smiled. The sardines could be deferred yet again for an emergency.

He heard the gate at the front of the compound creak open, then clang closed. A minute later a half dozen crabs ducked into their warrens as a small man carrying a gray plastic shopping bag entered the yard. He peered from under the brim of a white cowboy hat into the branches of the first mango tree, then walked to the second tree and peered, then to the third. He jumped, caught the end of a low branch, then jumped again still holding the branch and landed with a mango in his other hand. He dropped the fruit into his bag and walked out of sight around the back of the building.

Renati went to his room and spent ten minutes searching for his jackknife. He remembered cleaning it after making a sandwich at a lonely roadside bus stop, then closing it and setting it beside him on the rough-sawn bench. Yesterday? Some lucky bus passenger now possessed a good blade, he acknowledged without objection. He went to the kitchen and spent five minutes searching for a cutting tool, again to no avail. He returned to his room and used his camp fork to messily divide his breakfast more or less into quarters. He took his wallet from his handlebar bag and his pen from his wallet and made a list on the back of a hotel receipt:

jackknife

water taxi to SP, hotel reservation

groceries

direction: Honduras? Guatemala?

organize panniers

post office

short-sleeve shirt, swim trunks?

Rocinante bath, lube

haircut

sew socks

He texted the hotel manager for the Internet password and accepted her offer to take him shopping at three, then emptied his panniers onto the spare bed and set aside his sweater, windbreaker, black camp pants, and wool cap for mailing back to the States. He hadn't worn the sweater since Fort Davis and the windbreaker since Galveston, and was unlikely to need them again until

Quito or Lima, but for some reason he had been reluctant to relegate them to storage. He suspected he may have been hoping for a cool day.

IT ALWAYS TOOK HIM A MILE or more to adapt to the handling characteristics of a naked bicycle. It turned too quickly, accelerated too easily, braked too suddenly, and was utterly disinclined to keel over when standing still. Once he was reacquainted with its nimble nature, however – and once the handlebars stopped wobbling – he rode half again as fast in gears several ratios higher with an unaltered expenditure of effort. It felt, he thought, more like an idea than a machine. The relationship between muscles and road became magically integrated; the conversion of pedal rotations into forward motion seemed instantaneous.

He passed Brodie's Supermarket and spent forty minutes streaking through Belize City neighborhoods – banking through parking lots and dodging potholes – U-turning sharply on dead-end streets – drafting a twosome in matching team jerseys the length of Fabers Road south of the Western Highway – before circling back to the store. He bought eggs and bread for French toast, a quart each of orange juice and chocolate milk, coffee, assorted fresh vegetables, twelve ounces of good honey and sixteen of suspiciously pallid creamy peanut butter, and, on impulse, a box of his boyhood-favorite breakfast cereal.

He won't eat it. He hates everything! he recalled with a smile.

Prices, even for local fruit, were high. He drank his chocolate milk while loading his pantry bag and left-rear pannier, unchained Rocinante from a steel signpost, and pedaled to his hotel in heat and humidity that seemed to be increasing by the minute. He washed and lubricated Rocinante, undertook to repair one of his new cycling socks' defective stitching but stuffed it into his tool kit instead, shaved and showered, and wrote in his journal. In the company of the hotel manager and her son he bought swim shorts and a polo shirt at a downtown department store, then treated his hosts to supper at a Chinese restaurant. He retired to his concrete chamber and watched for the third or fourth time, *Man on Fire*.

Tomorrow he would reserve a kitchenette room in San Pedro and buy a seat on the water taxi, write a few letters, ride to the post office with outgoing mail, and give himself a haircut. The following afternoon he would cross to Ambergris Caye.

"I'm sorry you can't go," he said in the dark to his bicycle.

THE MANGO-GATHERER'S NAME was Bartolo. He was thirty-three, a former Guatemalan school teacher employed as hotel grounds-keeper and handyman from eight to six, six days a week, for ten American dollars a day. He had kind eyes and a shy smile. During a lunch-hour exchange of half-speed Spanish and overemphasized English – interspersed unhelpfully with pantomime that had both of them perplexed and laughing – he showed Renati how to select the best mangoes, breadfruit, craboo, and sapodilla, all of which grew on the hotel grounds. He lived in a sheet-metal hut with three other Guatemalan men in a squalid settlement between Haulover Creek and the Western Highway, an hour's walk from the hotel. He sent most of his pay home to a wife and daughter he hadn't seen in four months.

It was Bartolo's conscientious character and calm resolve that inspired Renati to ride west into Guatemala rather than south to Punta Gorda, Puerto Barrios, and Honduras, despite the warnings he had heard time and again in Mexico.

"*No vayas a Guatemala.*"

Or possibly, he thought, because of them.

WHEN A MENNONITE COUPLE at the post office informed Renati that flights to San Pedro were reasonably priced and that the municipal airport was only a few blocks from his hotel, he decided to fly. He boarded a Maya Island Air four-seater at two thirty the next day, landed on the caye twenty-five minutes later, and by three thirty checked into his room. He was the first evening customer at the open-air restaurant under his balcony, and he intended to order only an appetizer and coffee, but he was glad he yielded to his waiter's suggestion of Belizean seafood stew. As chairs filled and the cheerful din of vacationing diners heightened, he recalled a familiar Loggins and Messina song and wondered if he might be staying at *that* Holiday Hotel.

He climbed the stairs to his room and found a text message on his phone sent four hours earlier, while he was on the plane.

Hola, Michael, it read. *I am in San Pedro at a hostel that is not so good. Too many men make advances. Where are you?*

He glanced at the second double bed with the contents of his day pack spread across it, and replied: *Hola, Abelle. San Pedro. Here until Saturday. You can have the extra bed in my room. I promise no advances.*

He considered adding a smiley face but sent it without. He was asleep when his phone beeped with her response: *Really? What hotel? I will pay half.*

THEY MET AT ONE THIRTY in the hotel lobby. He declined her offer of payment for the room, but when she inspected the apartment-size kitchen and offered to buy groceries and cook their meals, he agreed. When she slipped into her bed that night wearing black silk tap pants and a clingy cotton T-shirt, he reminded himself of his promise.

She shopped early the next morning and prepared breakfast, which they ate seated on wicker chairs on the balcony overlooking the beach. He took an exploratory walk the length of Coconut Drive while she went job hunting. Her excitement about the possibility of life against a backdrop of tropical palms, sand, and sea – which had never particularly appealed to him – was contagious. They had pasta for supper and discussed her interview with a clothier on Barrier Reef Drive, then washed dishes together.

About an hour after dark she emerged from the bathroom wearing a swimsuit and sandals, her hair drawn into a bun and a hotel towel draped over one shoulder. Her suit was a backless one-piece with teal-and-turquoise palm branches crisscrossed in layers over white.

"Will you come with me swimming?" she asked.

It was a simple-enough question, but it took a moment for

him to reply.

"Okay."

"*Très bon*," she said. She was seated at the edge of her bed with the towel across her knees when he came out of the bathroom wearing his new swim shorts.

"I know," he said in response to her grin. "It's an unusual tan."

His arms were brown, and although his shoulders and torso had tanned somewhat in Mahahual, his new swim trunks were shorter than his cycling tights, resulting in a two-inch-wide stripe of sun-forsaken thigh. His extra-dark leg tan ended three inches above his ankles.

"You're wearing white socks," she observed.

"You can laugh if you want," he said. "But it took a lot of miles on a bicycle to achieve this . . . pattern."

She stood and tossed her towel back over her shoulder. "It is unusual," she said, her smile widening beneath fingers pressed to her lips, "but I'm not laughing."

Nineteen

"What would your life be like now if she hadn't left?" Abelle asked in the quiet of their room.

He marked his place with the owl feather he had carried since finding it on the Interstate near Lordsburg, New Mexico, and closed *Flint's Truth*. He turned to her across the four-foot gap separating their beds. She was inclined against pillows propped between her back and the wooden headboard, attired in her black sleep shorts and a matching camisole. A pale floral-print duvet hugged her legs. Baby-blue sheer curtains wavered across the dark window above the headboard.

"I'm going to stop the ceiling fan, okay?" she inquired. She pivoted from beneath the covers and walked to the wall switch by the front door. "Okay?" she asked again.

"Sure," he said.

He watched her return to her bed and rearrange her pillows, then lie to face him on her left side with the sheet pulled up under her right arm. They had talked after swimming about everything from travel and careers to movies and relationships, then said goodnight without switching off the lamp on the small table between their beds. She had busied herself with her phone and he had opened the last paper-paged book he would read before employing his leather-cased ebook reader, still empty.

"Do you mean if our marriage was what I thought it was?" he asked.

"Oui," she answered, nodding, her large brown eyes reflecting the lamplight. "It's okay to ask?"

"Of course," he said.

"Okay."

"Well," he began, "it's been almost four years since I got the email that said she'd hired a lawyer and that I should 'let her go,' so, if those years had –"

"Wait," Abelle interrupted. "She told you by an email? She didn't tell you at your face?"

"No."

"Were you separated?"

"Not in that way. I was building our home in Montana while she managed a hotel restaurant and bar in a resort town eight hours away. It was a temporary. We thought it would be better than making less money close to home and getting a loan to finish our house."

"Was it her idea?"

"No. Mine."

"Really? Do you have regret?"

"I can't regret it. She was unhappy at work and she wasn't being paid enough."

"So you wanted her to be happy."

"Every day of every year we were together. I also wanted her to be appreciated."

"Were *you* happy? What was her background?"

"I was very happy. Everything we had dreamed and planned for twenty years was finally within reach – though I never doubted it would be. She was a waitress when we met. After we married she worked as a bank teller, aerobics instructor, topless dancer, restaurant manager –"

"Topless . . . dancer?" Abelle asked.

Renati laughed. "Exotic dancer. Stripper."

"Really? You let her do that?"

"Sure. It was a decent club and she wanted to try it. And she made a lot of money."

"You're not a jealous person?"

"I'm not an insecure person. After a while the manager hired me as head doorman, and after a while the owner asked me to replace the manager. It was a bizarre job for someone who doesn't drink and doesn't like bars, but it paid extremely well and we earned more money in three years than we'd hoped to make in seven."

"Plus you got to see naked women all day!" Abelle exclaimed with a muted laugh.

"Half naked," Renati corrected. "That's what *topless* means."

"Was there trouble?"

"At the club? Some. But by the time I had the security staff I wanted confrontations were rare."

"Nobody wants to make a fight with a big guy?"

"No," he chuckled. "That wasn't it. Picking a fight with a big guy is one way to look tough in front of your friends."

Abelle was smiling. Her eyes shone.

"What?" Renati asked.

"Nothing. It's just . . . interesting. Different."

He nodded. "Crazy-loud music, booze flowing like a river, cigarette smoke, clashing perfumes, dollar bills everywhere, bare skin everywhere, and on Friday and Saturday nights a line out the door. But you asked what my life would be if . . ."

He fell silent.

She waited, then asked quietly, "Do you miss her?"

"No. Well," he added, "I miss who I thought she was, who I thought we were together. It still seems unreal that she abandoned our marriage the way she did, as if she had been leaving for months or years and then just one day decided to tell me. Actually, she didn't even do that. Something she said made me take a step back and I found myself wondering if her priorities had changed."

"What did she say?"

"She called our dog, *your* dog. And he was *our* dog. But, your question, if our life was . . ."

She waited. After a long pause he said, "I thought I knew then, but I didn't. So I really can't speculate now." He smiled faintly, reflectively, and said, "She told me I taught her how to think. She asked me to build a tango pavilion on our property so we could host outdoor dances on summer nights."

Abelle sat up straight and faced him. The covers fell around her waist. "You are a tango dancer?" she asked.

"We were students of Argentine tango, yes."

"Are you angry at her?"

He shook his head. "She told a mutual friend she thought I should be. But, no. Disappointed."

"That she left?"

"That she left as if our marriage no longer served her, as if it had brought her to where she wanted to be and was done with it."

In the silence that followed, Abelle said, "I'm sorry."

He looked at her lovely face and neck and shoulders, at her fingers extended gracefully on the bed linens bunched around her hips, and nodded. He wanted to say that he found her beautiful and attractive, that he was glad she was sharing his room and that perhaps he had spoken too hastily when promising no advances.

"Thank you, Abelle," he said. "I'll see you in the morning."

RENATI CONCLUDED THE BUSINESS that brought him to San Pedro and assisted Abelle with revising her resumé in English. On the eve of her return to the mainland they watched *L'Empire des Loups* lying side by side on his bed with his computer on his knees. The movie was produced in French with English subtitles – one reason he thought she might enjoy it – but she did not enjoy it. He walked with her to the dock in the morning for her departure to Corozal, where she would continue by bus back to Cancún. When she returned from the ticket window she stood on tiptoe and kissed his cheek.

"Why didn't you make a pass at me?" she asked.

"I said I wouldn't," he answered, not expecting the question. "I didn't want you to worry about staying with me, and I wanted you to stay with me."

As he spoke he realized there was another reason he had not yielded to the desire he felt for her, but it was a reason he would not fully understand until many months later. It was enough, he knew, that he had given his word.

She kissed him again, took a step back, and smiled.

"Thank you, Michael," she said. "I'll text from Cancún. Okay?"

"Please do."

"*Au revoir.*"

"*Au revoir,* Abelle."

Twenty

He needed to ride, and to ride fast. To swerve between cars and dodge road debris and race traffic lights and outrun dogs. He packed his bag, returned to the dock, traded his Belize-to-San Pedro water-taxi ticket for one back to the mainland, and arrived at his hotel with three hours of daylight remaining. He plucked socks, shorts, and a jersey from the paracord clothesline strung across his bathroom. He dressed, strapped MICA to his pantry bag, and ran his bicycle down the hall and down the stairs and streaked into downtown Belize City with burning legs and lungs.

"Did you miss me?" he asked Rocinante.

He peddled furiously for twenty minutes – sprinting and veering, sprinting and braking – squinting through the sweat that ran into his eyes and splashed his sunglasses. He paid no mind to street names or to the ground he was covering or to the stares he received. When he banked into a left-hand turn and realized he was riding the wrong way on a one-way he swerved into the parking lot of an apartment building and, when an odd gray shape between residents' cars caught his attention, he stopped abruptly, dismounted, and backed Rocinante several steps while withdrawing his camera from his handlebar bag. Without looking through the viewfinder he pressed the shutter release twice.

Curled into itself like a charcoal comma was a large dog unlike any he had ever seen. Its coat was short except in random patches where it bristled in a wispy crest up its spine. The top of its head and the tips of its ears were encrusted with scaly whitish ulcers. The pathetic hound had too much skin.

"Damn," Renati whispered. "What happened to you?"

The dog lifted its head and their eyes met, then it slowly, almost apologetically, looked away. Renati glanced left and right for a place to lean his bicycle. The dog began to stand.

"Please," Renati implored, "don't go. I promise it's okay."

The dog hesitated in a tired sitting position and waited while Renati snapped a third picture, as if waiting was what it could offer in return for a kind voice. When Renati laid his bicycle on the ground the animal stood, and with its sad head lowered and its rat-like tail tucked, it awkwardly climbed over the high curb against which it had been lying and vanished silently under a corrugated fence panel.

"Wait," Renati called.

The fence was too tall to see over and the ground too strewn with broken glass to kneel and look underneath.

"I'll be here tomorrow with food," he said into the place where the dog had retreated, his eyes filling with tears. "And," he said to himself, "a name."

He stopped at a park on Barrack Road and then at an Indian restaurant on Baymen, and cycled the dark mile back to his hotel with his flashlight strapped to his left palm. In the morning he bought a pound of beef franks and returned to where he had seen the dog. He spent an hour searching side streets, yards, fence lines, and parking lots, sometimes riding, sometimes walking. Once, he thought he saw a canine beneath a rickety house on creosote-treated posts, but when he called to the apparition it blended into the shadows. While riding through a narrow garbage-littered alley he was confronted by a raggedy quartet of aggressive men. He dismounted and bisected the group on foot with his right palm resting on MICA's side handle, ignoring their taunts, all of a sudden aware that even the food he was carrying might be, in such a neighborhood, worth trying to steal.

After parking Rocinante in his room he put the franks in the hotel refrigerator for Bartolo. The next morning, as he detoured through downtown on his way out of the city, he shouted as loud as he could on the street where he had met the dog:

"Your name is Argos!"

Twenty One

The nearer he got to the Belize Zoo the more Belize looked like Africa, not that he had been to Africa. The country opened into grassy plains dotted with a mix of low palm-like vegetation and rangy long-needle pines. Delineating the skyline to the southwest was a jagged hazy-blue ridge. An occasional solitary conifer stood like an emaciated sentinel silhouetted against a cloud-dappled firmament. Periodic patches of brown suggested sun scorching or grass-fire scars.

Could Africa be any hotter? he wondered.

He turned south off the Western Highway onto an earthen trail that descended gradually to, he hoped, the zoo's Tropical Education Center, where he had reserved a cabin for two nights. Except for motor-vehicle tracks he saw no evidence of habitation, but eventually the trail brought him to a landscaped enclave of tidy buildings, signs, footpaths, and busy humans. He found the office and paid for his accommodations, and was escorted by a young man across an elevated wooden walkway to a small cabin over a shallow lagoon. What he assumed to be fish drifting languidly beneath the water's surface were, he saw after looking more closely, baby crocodiles.

He parked Rocinante on the screened porch, inspected his rustic room-and-a-half, and returned to the office to request another two nights' lodging.

He walked to the zoo the morning after his arrival and finished his self-guided tour under the first drops of a pelting downpour. The inspiring accounts he had read did not exaggerate: it was a wonder-filled experience. He ordered lunch in the cafeteria about a minute before it filled with drenched-to-the skin visitors, and returned to his cabin through wet grass under intermittent sun by way of the sedately rolling open country south of the Center's access road.

That afternoon, while sitting on his porch in a plastic deck chair, his journal open in one hand and a mugful of fresh-brewed coffee in the other, he heard a gentle swishing sound almost directly beneath him. As he leaned forward and focused through the screen, his gaze met the steady flat stare of a seven-foot-long crocodile floating in a green bed of ropy underwater plants. Every few seconds the prehistoric creature's tail swept left in the water, then right.

He had been assured that only juvenile crocodiles inhabited the pond – but what did he know about the growth rate of crocodiles?

"You look hungry," he observed, exchanging his coffee for the camera on the chair beside him. He glanced to his right at Rocinante, then back at the crocodile. "Oh, no –" he said sternly, "you leave my bicycle alone."

BREAKFAST IN THE CENTER'S DINING ROOM the following morning was a pandemonium with students excited for the next stop on their tour: Belize's Great Blue Hole. A threesome of teenaged American girls asked if they could sit in the empty chairs at Renati's table for four. Two chattered nonstop, sometimes with each other, sometimes with girls at the table behind them. They talked about cell phones and boyfriends and the other girls and their chaperons, and about tan lines and hair highlights and being seniors and a television program that apparently followed the daily life of some quirky family. Renati soon found himself imagining a game where observers could compete for a prize by counting how many topics of discussion were begun and forgotten. The third girl remained silent behind wire-framed glasses, sitting with her hands clasped over a spiral-bound notebook in her lap.

He had almost finished the last of his scrambled eggs when a fourth girl with wet blonde hair approached and said to the talkative two, "Hey, guys! Can I pull up a chair?"

Renati raised his hand to get the standing girl's attention and indicated his place. "Sit here," he said. The silent girl looked up at him when he rose to leave. Her mouth formed the word, *Sorry*. He smiled at her and replied silently, *That's okay*.

He returned to his cabin and passed through the porch to where he had hung last night's laundry. He unclipped what was dry and brought it inside and tossed it on his bed. He reached for his left-front pannier leaning on the floor against the bathroom wall, then paused.

It was time, he decided, to complete the task he had begun in Belize City.

He unfastened and unzipped each of his pannier's compartments and placed the contents neatly in four rectangles on his bed. He did the same for his handlebar and pantry bags, then straightened and stepped back to examine his inventory. He laughed, recalling a line from *The Princess Bride*.

"Plus my brains and your strength," he declared through the door to Rocinante. He frowned at his camping gear and tallied its weight: twelve pounds unused since Texas.

He had considered and rejected two semi-discreet tent sites along his Yucatan route. The first, between Tulum and Felipe Carrillo Puerto, was over a muddy steep berm and a hundred meters down a two-rut track that ended in a clearing carpeted with garbage. By the time he had prepared a spot away from the mess, his neck, legs, and arms were stippled with mosquito bites, he was soaked with sweat, and the soles of his shoes were heavy with gluey mud. The second, between Crooked Tree and Sand Hill, was sufficiently hidden from the road in a tidy citrus orchard, but the ground was spongy and it was too early in the day to stop riding. He seemed to have decided without deciding that a shower and cool sheets and a sink for washing clothes – plus the time saved not setting and breaking camp – was worth the small amount he was spending each night.

"Better to have you and not need you," he said to his tent.

He separated his computer from the arrangement and re-packed his bags and returned them in a standing row against the bathroom wall. He boiled water on the cabin's hot plate and made

Earl Grey tea with honey, then popped a memory card from a waterproof case and brought it with his tea and computer to the porch. The machine was slow to boot, but it was compact and adequate to his needs. A three-pound folder able to transport a library of writing, art, and entertainment hardly deserved criticism, he thought. He waited, sipping his tea and scanning the lagoon for crocodiles.

"I know," he said to Rocinante. "I can be slow to process certain things, too."

He spent the next five hours with letters, notes, photographs and video clips, and music not in his players. How valuable it could be, he was reminded not for the first time, to inventory one's past. How easy it could be to forget or take for granted not only the minutiae of one's history, but its defining moments.

The process, he thought, was like looking in a mirror that reached back across time. He wondered if it was normal to experience clipped-and-saved fragments of life not as reminiscences, but practically, as lessons upon which to build what a mirror could not show. He felt nostalgia with some of his music – remembering places and times and people interwoven with lyrics and chords – and with some of his photographs, but with every sentence he had written, no matter what the subject, he was revisiting himself as a witness.

He recalled a line from Ann Morrow Lindbergh's journals about writing being more than living because it meant being conscious of living.

He reread correspondence with friends, memoranda to himself, and newspaper-opinion-column submissions. He reread, for about the fiftieth time, the letters that had resulted in and followed from the break with his family. He reread ninety cell-phone texts thumbed in predawn darkness across two and a half years of sleep interrupted by a question or realization about his marriage. He had sent the texts into the neverland of unread epistles until one day, when his outbox was full, he saved them to a file labeled *Kites*.

He read an assortment of essays and news articles copied and set aside for a later date, and studied his scan of a South America map marked with route options and notes about weather and roads. He reviewed his Last Will and Testament, then bagged his computer and spent the remainder of the afternoon roaming the Center's nature trail.

TWO MORNINGS LATER he departed for San Ignacio. His cabin had been reserved for an arriving group, so he spent his last night sleeping poorly under a pedestal fan on the library floor. At the start of a long straightaway into Belmopan he enjoyed a second breakfast packed for him by the girls in the Center's kitchen. He queued thirty-seven minutes of Fogelberg so that he might, if he kept his pace, coast into the capital city before the final guitar strum in "Bones in the Sky." It played as he passed the entrance to the Hector Silva Airstrip.

On the other side of Belmopan, in front of a store set back from the road, he saw a hand-painted wooden sign that read, "Hom Made Chees." He bought a wax-paper-wrapped wedge and a bottle of orange juice. From patchy shade under trees at the edge of the dirt lot he watched a lanky man wearing a navy-blue suit coast in from the pavement on an old Schwinn ten speed, standing as he rode. The man dismounted and set his kick stand and walked into the store, then emerged a moment later with a newspaper folded under one arm. He climbed back over his bicycle, retracted his kick stand with the heel of a shiny shoe, and pedaled, again standing, toward Renati.

He braked and stopped a few feet away. He extended a bony ebony hand. "You've traveled far," he said. "What's your name?"

"Michael," Renati answered. "Yours?"

"Richard. Do you mind if I study your fine machine?"

Richard's skin was so dark the only features Renati could distinguish in the shade were his eyes and teeth and some gray at his temples. He admired Rocinante for a while, then said, "Never seen one like this. It's a good name. Had mine since it was new."

The Le Tour's yellow paint was chipped and dull. The cable housings were encircled with cracks and the chrome-plated chain-ring guard and spoke protector were rust-blotched. The drop bars, raised at least to maximum height, were wrapped with electrical and masking tape. Renati exhaled involuntarily when he noticed that the bicycle lacked a saddle: a deeply scratched steel seatpost rose dangerously, or maybe comically, from the seat tube.

"How long have you been without a saddle?" he asked.

Richard grinned brightly. "Long time, I guess. Somebody stole it. I s'pose I got used to not having one."

"You could remove the post. It would be safer, even if you like standing."

"Can't," said Richard. "Stuck."

He again extended his hand, and again Renati shook it.

"I'm glad I met you," Richard said, touching his newspaper to his perspiring brow and pedaling upright to the road and to wherever he was going in a suit. Renati finished his juice and circled back to the store to drop the bottle into a blue plastic drum with a sawed-off top.

He rode in quiet ease, reflectively, enjoying the whisper of his tires and the clean click of changing gears, not disliking the heat. He removed his helmet and hung it by the strap from a brake lever. He tucked the damp liner into his jersey's lower-back pocket and savored the relief of the breeze through his wet hair.

Near Teakettle just north of the highway, the Belize River, the Old River, meandered to the Atlantic from its origin out of the Macal and Mopan near San Ignacio. To the south Renati could see, like feathery pencil shadings slanted over the emerald edge of the distant Mayan Mountains, rain. Ahead, beyond an ever-nearing everchanging panorama, he studied a vision less tangible: clear at its center, undefined at its borders, indefinite in its distance.

Perhaps it had been the setting, perhaps the timing. Perhaps both had converged with what he was discovering and affirming about himself. Whatever the contributing determinants, in a picturesque cabin overlooking a crocodile lagoon on the Belize savannah, he had arrived at the crossroads inevitably encountered by all knights-errant, and his thousand-meter target had come into view.

Along the Way

Cancún . . . San Ignacio

Ten

Rocinante's boxcar

Except for a broken mirror, in fine fettle

East of Laguna Nichupté: Zona Hotelera

West of Laguna Nichupté: Zona de Cocodrilos

A modern Mayan maiden?

Eleven

An extra day in Tulum

Desayuno pequeño gratis

Twelve

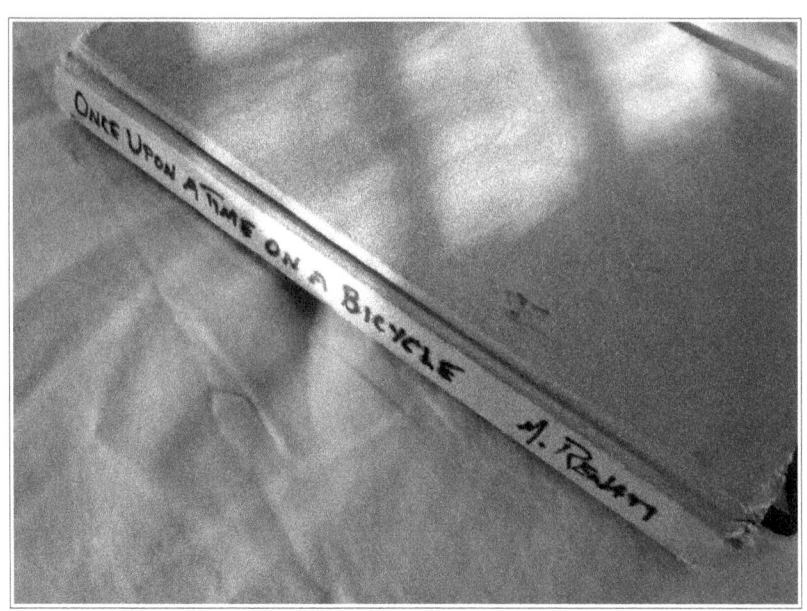

First Edition

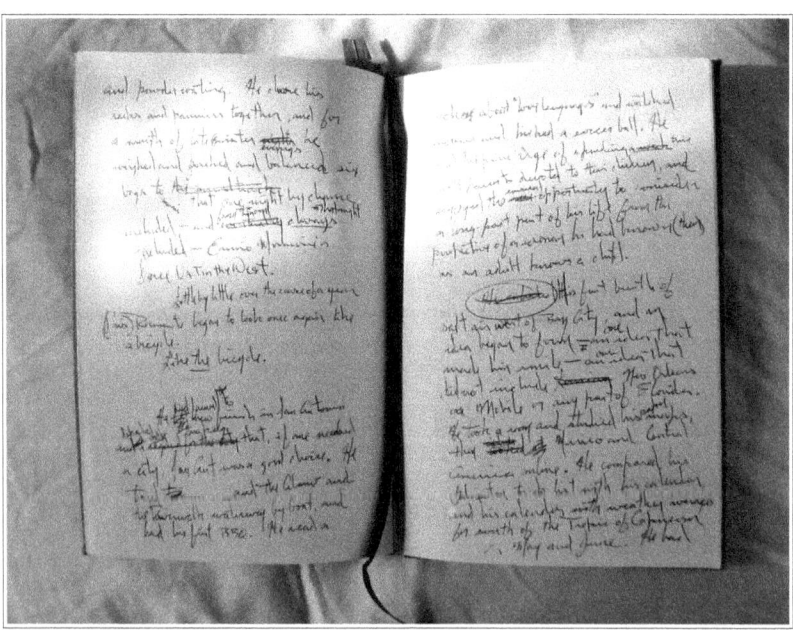

Thirteen

Muyil, originally Chunyaxché

A five hundred-year-old kind of quiet

Reclamation or integration?

Era verde el silencio, mojada era la luz   —Pablo Neruda

Continuing to Felipe Carrillo Puerto

Fourteen

Making the most of losing one's way in Felipe Carrillo Puerto

Stone and palm

Plumb as an average

Triciclo

Into the storm

A Costa Maya rain

End of the road

A Mahahual sunset

Could this be home?

Fifteen

Hotel Luna de Plata

Tuning Rocinante (B.R. photo)

Extra traction into a headwind

A decree does not make it so

A Bacalar bicycle trap

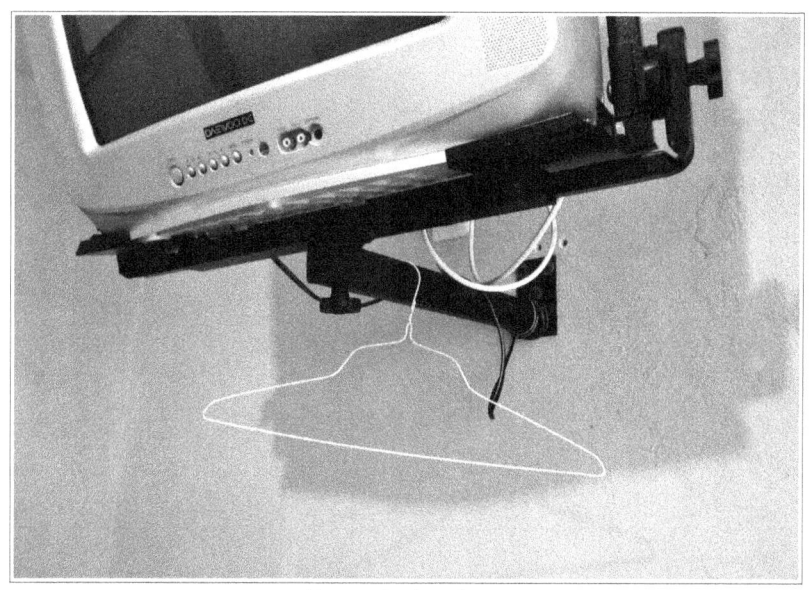

Hang clothes here

Approaching Chetumal

A topic for discussion

Welcome to Chetumal

Sixteen

Adios, Mexico

Hello, Belize

Seventeen

Guardian of the stairs

Cerros unvisited

Self-titled

Departing for Orange Walk Town (Gwyn Lawrence photo)

Take two (Gwyn Lawrence photo)

Better than a forked stick and worth the ride back

Cane-factory ruins on the road through Libertad

Orange Walk mud

An illusory break in the clouds

Bicycle art on the Northern Highway

The Belize River east of Ladyville

Eighteen

Downtown Belize City

Exploring side streets

Life above the appliance store

Belize City Post Office

Crossing to Ambergris Caye

Landing in San Pedro Town

Nineteen

A Barrier Reef vista

Barrier Reef Drive

Breakfast with Abelle

Lunch with an unexpected guest (Abelle C. photo)

La Isla Bonita

Twenty

. . . he wagged his tail and dropped both his ears, but nearer to his master he had no longer strength to move. —Homer

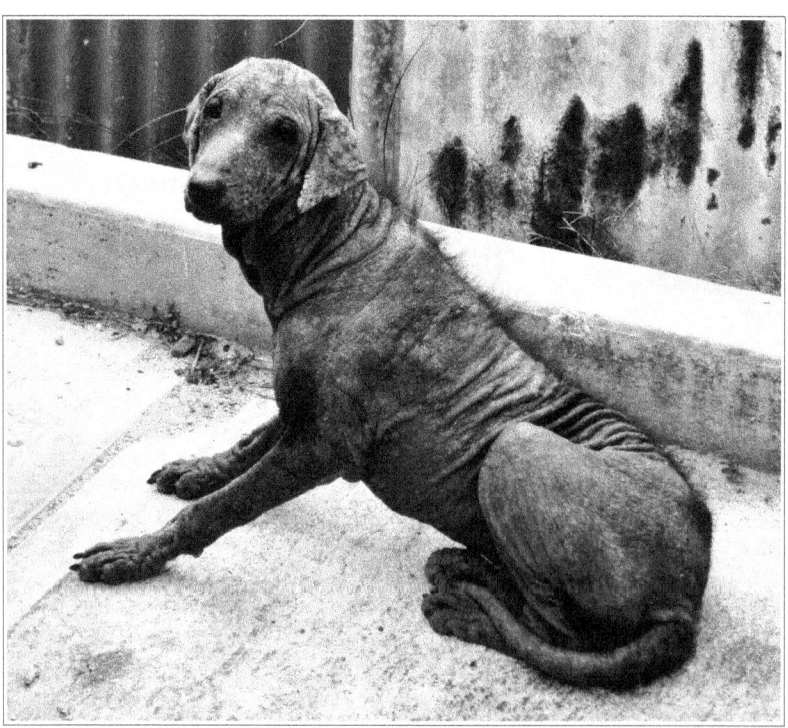

Twenty One

In the middle of nowhere with nothing on the other side

Southwest on the Western Highway

The trail to the Tropical Education Center

Belize savannah

For Gino Vannelli

Stranger, if you passing, meet me,
And desire to speak to me,
Why should you not speak to me?
And why should I not speak to you?

—Walter Whitman

Walkway to a cabin over a lagoon

Thank you, Sharon Matola, for the Belize Zoo and this place

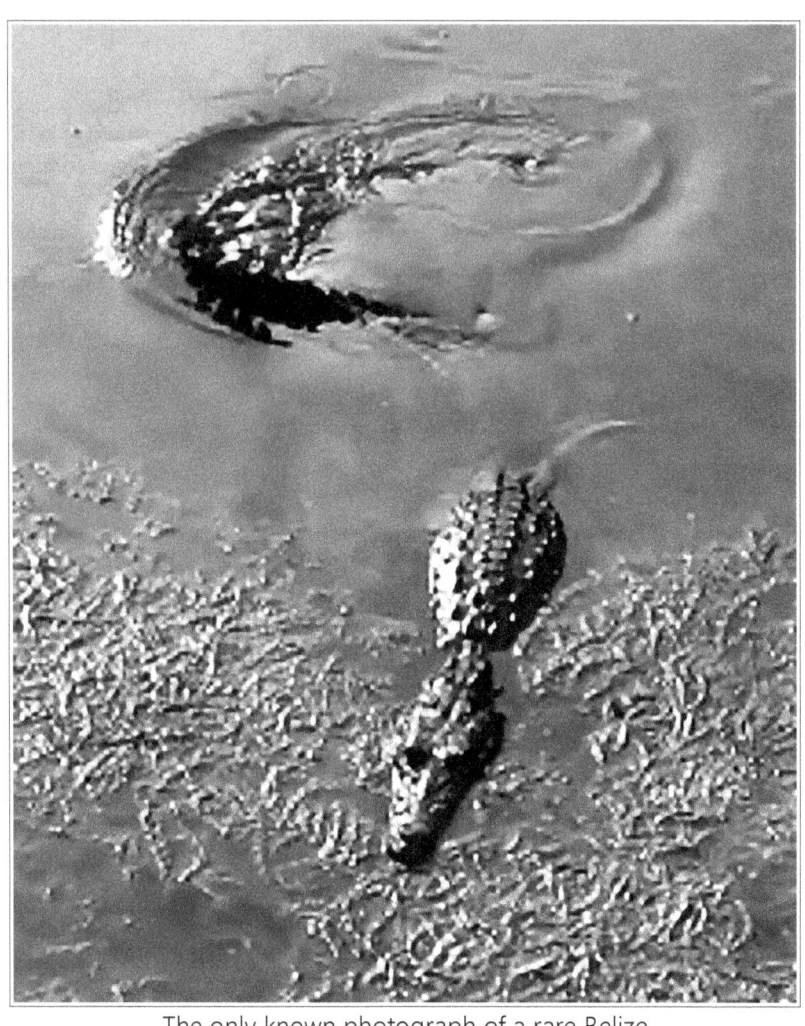

The only known photograph of a rare Belize bicycle-eating crocodile (Crocodylus moreletii birotatio)

Next stop, San Ignacio

STAGE THREE

The Road to La Mancha

Take the hard road, if it's the right road.

Flint's Truth
Richard S. Wheeler, 1998

Twenty Two

The restaurant's interior felt even narrower than its narrow facade suggested, with four small booths along the left wall and two on the right. The walls were painted concrete, one side off-white, the other pale blue, displaying an odd variety of framed prints, unframed posters, narrow wooden shelves collecting unrelated objects, and leafy stenciling. There was a small tube-type television mounted at a downward angle in one corner, switched off. Bare fluorescent bulbs in two single-strip ceiling fixtures illuminated what the mid-morning light from the west-facing windows didn't reach, but the booth at the back shone in the glimmer of a red Coca-Cola cooler beside it. In the booth sat a woman with a white mug in one hand and a book in the other. Across from her was the only unoccupied seat in the establishment.

She looked up from her book, placed it pages-side down on the table, and motioned for Renati to join her.

He wanted neither company nor conversation, but he had been hungry since waking at seven and eating a few crumbs of granola and the last of his dried fruit, and this was the only breakfast restaurant he had seen after walking the streets of San Ignacio for half an hour. He glanced at the food on the table nearest the front: fried eggs with bacon, a plate-size waffle, fruit-garnished pancakes, a stack of puffy fried pastries, pulpy orange juice, and coffee. According to the sign painted on one of the twin front doors, a bottomless cup.

He walked to the woman's booth, exchanged introductions, and placed an order for coffee and banana pancakes. Breakfast was excellent, and he enjoyed their conversation until she answered his question about the scar on her neck.

IT WOULD BE A LONG DAY, he thought, longer than what his map indicated. He looked at his watch. Five kilometers into Guatemala with another sixty to El Remate and it was already past noon. He sipped ninety-degree water from his second bottle.

The border crossing had been farcical, as if the process had originated in someone's garage and expanded to a second garage, then a third. He knew that Belize imposed an "exit fee" but he had not considered the silliness of it until the agent asked him to pay.

Or what? he had wondered, *I have to stay here?* A tourist-visa charge upon entering a country was at least explicable, but a pay-to-leave toll?

He had also read that he would be charged an "unofficial" fee to enter Guatemala and that most people paid it, but his decision not to pay was never tested. A Belizean immigration officer told him that the Guatemalan office was on the left just across the river; the money changer from whom he bought Guatemalan *quetzales* told him it was on the right before the river. But there was nothing on the right before, and nothing on the left after, so he rode twice through downtown Melchor de Mencos searching. Probably, he wagered, it was farther in-country, like some of the crossings in Mexico.

It wasn't. He would learn several weeks later that it was on the right after the river across a drainage ditch in a rusty-roofed shed marked by hand-painted lettering on clapboard siding.

He was sitting under partly cloudy skies on a low bank beside the eastbound lane of CA-13, wondering why he felt slightly . . . what?

Dejected? Despondent? Weary? Angry?

He sipped from a cup of warm strawberry yogurt while distractedly nibbling at a plain corn tortilla. Two black police pickup trucks with *Petén* printed in white across their tailgates drove past, followed by an uncovered Guatemala Army troop carrier with eight uniformed soldiers seated four to a side in the back. He saluted and two of the men returned the gesture.

He thought about what the woman in the restaurant had told

him. Was it was because he was a stranger that she had been so forthcoming? Or because she believed he could be trusted with a deeply personal story? Or had it just been time for her to tell *someone*?

He stood, brushed a few ants from his legs, and walked into the meadow behind the trees that lined the berm.

It was anger, he realized. Anger and helplessness – his most-despised emotional pairing. He wanted to hit something. No, not some *thing*. He wanted to feel a momentary resistance of flesh give way to structural trauma, damage, breakage. He clenched and unclenched his hands. He scanned the ground for something to throw. Through gritted teeth he growled an unsatisfactory, "Fuck!"

His childhood had been so clean, so simple. "Fucking perfect," he said to the meadow.

His parents were loving toward their four children and in love with each other. They were thoughtful, conscientious, responsible, productive, dedicated, and fun. They were kind and strict in equal measure, teaching values by example, encouraging independence and self-exploration, and supporting their children's interests. With the exception of a schoolmate whose father, it was rumored, hit the boy with his fists, Renati had been raised assuming that his was simply "the life of a young person," and taking it for granted. He knew that not all parents were intelligent, supportive, understanding, sober, or fair, but he was in his mid-thirties before he came face to face with the fact that life for some children was unimaginably wrong, and that the long-term consequences could be devastating.

He walked for a while longer through thick green grass and sparse wildflowers, attempting to convert his rage into something articulate, then he returned to his bicycle and slid his voice recorder's power switch to the *on* position. He put his empty yogurt cup into his empty tortilla package and zipped them into his pantry bag, clipped his left foot to the corresponding pedal and his microphone to his lapel, and pushed away from the gravel shoulder across to the westbound lane. He depressed the record button on his device but rode for several minutes before saying, slowly and with a bitter emphasis:

"It matters not who you are or what excuses you offer, you who have sexually abused a child have forfeited not only your right to raise, befriend, or ever again speak to a child, but your right to remain among the living. Your existence as a human person ended the moment you succumbed to whatever defect in your soul made such a depraved betrayal possible. There is nothing you can do to repent; nothing you can do to repay; nothing any pathetic doctrine of forgiveness can forgive. The only moral choice left to you is the one that removes you from the world of your victim. Parent or grandparent, uncle or aunt, sibling or neighbor: There is nothing any longer that can become your life like the self-directed leaving of it.

"End," he said.

He tucked the microphone and cord into the right-side mesh pocket of his handlebar bag, then slid the recorder's power switch to *off* and rode another thirty-six kilometers in silence. He stopped across the road from a blue-painted *comedor* in a village ten minutes west of El Zapote. He had ridden too far too fast on too few calories; he felt lightheaded. A shirtless boy of eight or nine sitting on the restaurant's steps stood and jumped the gutter and ran to Renati as he leaned Rocinante against a low concrete wall topped by a chain-link fence.

"*Eres de America?*" the boy asked when his inspection of the bicycle was finished. His round brown face was smudged with dirt and something orange.

"*Sí*," Renati answered. "But I think I will like Guatemala." He peeled off his right glove and extended his hand to the boy. "*Yo soy Miguel.*"

The boy took his hand and pulled and said, "*Vienes a comer ahora.*"

Twenty Three

He unpacked in the dark at Hotel Las Gardenias, purchased a tour of Tikal for the following morning, and ordered tilapia and a baked potato at the hotel restaurant. He washed his clothes in the sink and walked to an ATM, but the machine had an X of duct tape applied over the card slot. When returning to his room he noticed rows of white hotel towels hanging on a line beside a laundry outbuilding, and understood why his bath towel smelled of smoke.

Two shuttle buses arrived from Flores before sunup and climbed to Tikal through fleecy tiers of jungle fog. One passenger had assumed that the excursion price covered park admission and brought only enough cash to pay for lunch; another produced the needed currency and addresses were exchanged. The tour of the vast archaeological site, led by a knowledgeable local guide named Luis, was a marvel. For Renati, the highlight of the day was learning that undistinguished jungle-overgrown hillocks were not, as he might have supposed, natural topographic features, but unexcavated man-made stone edifices. He hadn't noticed that he was the only solo traveler until, standing with his group on a windswept ledge near the top of Temple IV, he found himself taking pictures of couples and friends with friends.

He lingered an extra two hours scouting less-traveled paths, and spent thirty minutes stalking nowhere-to-be-seen crocodiles from the bank of a muddy crocodile pond. While waiting in an open-air eatery for the last shuttle to El Remate, he joined a young Danish couple discussing their collection of vintage American television shows. They had so far acquired episodes from *I Love Lucy, The Beverly Hillbillies, Get Smart, Gilligan's Island, The Adams*

Family, *Mash*, *My Three Sons*, and *Bewitched*. Renati recommended *The Twilight Zone* and *Bonanza* and wanted to tell them about his favorite, but kept it to himself.

IT WAS A BLUSTERY mid-November afternoon when Daisy June's little sister asked, "Did you have a hero when you were growing up? Like, when you were my age?"

She was eight, four years younger than Daisy June, adorable, happy, whimsically inquisitive, and of the two the less inclined to proffer a serious question. She fancied earrings and fingernail polish and seemed in a hurry to be nine. Or fifteen. She rested one pink-nailed hand on Ragnar's back and waited. Daisy June had stopped in the path and turned, also waiting.

"I did," Renati answered, "and I guess I was about your age."

He motioned for the girls to continue walking. Ragnar trotted ahead.

"There was a television show that came on – I think every weeknight – at five thirty. They were reruns. Do you know what reruns are?"

Daisy June said, "Yes." Her sister nodded.

"It was about a rancher in New Mexico Territory in the 1800s. He had a son named Mark. His wife, Mark's mother, had died of smallpox when they lived in Oklahoma so he was raising the boy alone. He was a good man, honest and fair, and a protector."

"What's that?" the younger girl asked.

"Someone who keeps you safe," her sister replied.

"He was a friend to good people and dangerous to bad people. Almost every episode had a lesson about right and wrong. My parents must have approved because supper always waited until after the program was over."

"Did they watch it with you?" Daisy June asked.

"I don't remember. I think my dad sometimes caught the last ten or fifteen minutes when he got home from work. Mark's father reminded me of my dad. They were both tall men, strong, quiet, gentle but tough."

"What was his name?" the girls asked at the same time.

Renati smiled, poignantly aware of what those stories had meant to him, unaware that it would be years before he fully understood how profoundly and everlastingly they had shaped him.

"Lucas McCain," he said.

HE LIKED GUATEMALA.

The ubiquitous acrid smoke from burning garbage somehow harmonized with thatch-roofed stick huts and miniature tin-topped concrete homes, and it didn't seem to affect him adversely. The political banners and paintings that adorned nearly every vertical surface – business and house walls, fences, utility poles, cliff faces, roadside boulders – left him searching for words to describe his response to the phenomenon.

It was bizarre, ugly, and garish – but not merely so. In the United States of America political advertising was a slick display of professionally marketed bromides. In Guatemala it was just the unadorned sordid reality of contemporary politics.

Tacky but genuine, he decided.

He liked the roads, the truck drivers, the people he met, the jungle, and the nearly complete lack of spoken English. He was becoming almost comfortable in the heat. There was something intriguing about the poverty, something that made him want to explore, understand, compare it with life in The Land of Debt and Excess. He was surprised to see so many roadside-village dwellers talking on cellular phones. They might have poor houses and they might be able to converse with their neighbors through glassless windows, but there was no shortage of cell phones.

He had been prepared to ride through Guatemala at a sprint in response to warnings offered by acquaintances in Mexico and Belize, but if El Petén was a fair example of what he could expect, the country was going to be a pleasure to cross at a leisurely pace. Two leisurely rainy days south of Lago Petén Itzá, he quartered Rocinante in a bungalow on a jungle farm that inspired him to consider not *crossing* Guatemala, but *staying* in Guatemala.

Twenty Four

Finca Ixobel, a jungle farm-cum-traveler's rest south of Poptún, exemplified the best-possible definition of *special*. In 1971, Michael and Carole DeVine journeyed through Mexico and Belize from California in search of farmland, which they found and purchased in the nearly inaccessible northern jungles of Guatemala. As the arduous primitive-road trek from Guatemala City to Flores and Tikal improved with the demands of tourist travel, so did the demand for civilized accommodations en route. The DeVine's reputation for providing good food and a place to camp led to the creation of a farmstead restaurant and hotel-quality amenities on manicured grounds surrounded by emerald wilderness.

Renati felt more in his element at Finca Ixobel than in any other place through which he had yet ridden. The haven's distance from town and welcoming forest-lane access, its thoughtfully designed self-sufficiency, the calm that prevailed even with guests coming and going, and, perhaps especially, the wonder of discovering such a place in such a place, filled him with a sense of admiration and belonging. While reading about the finca's history, however, he came upon a sentence both incongruous and arcane.

"Unfortunately Michael DeVine passed away in 1990."

He found a *Los Angeles Times* report online that described the worst-possible definition of *unfortunately*.

> It has been gut-wrenching enough, trying to reconcile the death of their father in a Guatemalan pine forest, his body, all but decapitated, leaning against the back tire of his Ford Club Wagon....

He looked away and took a deep breath. He pushed his half-eaten supper aside. The report continued, detailing the DeVine's development of their hostelry, the day Michael was last seen alive, the search by family and friends, an uncooperative police and military, the discovery of Michael's body, the local-court conviction of five soldiers and a captain of the Guatemalan army, and allegations that a United States Central Intelligence Agency-paid informant was responsible for the murder.

He closed his computer and pushed his chair back from the outdoor dining table. He brought his plate and silverware to the kitchen and returned to his bungalow. He tried to compose in his journal but after fifty minutes all he had written – opposite a map he had sketched to show an inquiring Belizean boy from whence he had bicycled – was *Colonel Julio Roberto Alpirez*. He returned to the finca kitchen for a bottle of mineral water and listened to an audiobook that finally, two hours later, led him to sleep.

IT HAD BEEN THREE YEARS since he had experienced the only recurring dream of his life, the dream that had been the start of his predawn awakenings and one-way text kites, but it visited him again that night. He knew it was a dream and he thought he could wake from it if he chose, but he let it play. It hadn't changed.

She was riding her bicycle on the far side of a busy city street when he saw her struck by a car. It took too long in the heavy traffic for him to reach the place where she fell, and there remained only her bicycle and blood and a policeman who gripped his holstered pistol and asked, "Are you Michael?" He searched every hospital in every town in which they had ever lived until he glimpsed her through the window of a closed door, much older, asleep in a bed with her hand on a book. He wanted to enter the room and read to her but the door was locked. Her sister's face appeared in the window. He showed her a photograph of the house he built but the woman said, "She's happy now," and pulled a curtain across the glass.

He opened his eyes and turned onto his back and scrutinized the shadowy wooden trusswork over his bed. He had scarcely been a participant in their divorce. She had permitted no discussion, no counseling, no "going back" as she called it. She had even expected him to sign and return by mail her divorce document, rather than face each other with the mutual deference he believed had characterized their marriage. When he arrived at the meeting place designated by her lawyer, he saw a policeman hiding behind a van on the street and was addressed by name by officers at the door who scanned and frisked him. Through a surreal incredulity he observed a procedure officially over long before the reality of it reached him, as if their life together never happened.

Worse, he admitted reluctantly: as if their life together never mattered.

AT THE SOUTHEAST CORNER of the finca, at the terminus of a jungle-canopied footpath, was a small stream-fed pond. He had ventured there twice – last night in a thunderstorm and this afternoon in filmy sunshine. He sat at one end of a single-plank bench under a crown-heavy pumpo tree. At the opposite end of the bench rested the vessel he had crafted out of a broken board, a forked sapling, tropical foliage, and a candle stub. There was a mild westerly breeze. The sky was suffused with cobwebby clouds. He could hear in the distance a chainsaw-wielding worker clearing the tree that had fallen in front of his bungalow during the storm. From a pocket in his cargo shorts he removed a pen, two folded sheets of white paper, and two wooden matches. He placed the pen and matches on the bench and unfolded the papers.

Silently from the first sheet he read their self-composed wedding vows, then pressed his lips to the paper and crumpled it into a ball and placed it beside the candle in the little green boat. He smoothed the second sheet between his palms and stood to face the pond. He read aloud:

"I honored you as my greatest friend. I worshiped you as my lover. I respected you as my equal. I stood at your side in all that you did as the man you chose to be your husband. I swore by my life and by my love of it to do these things, and in the name of the best within me I kept my promise. I loved you, and I knew what that meant.

"On this day at Finca Ixobel in Guatemala, I release myself from the promise I made nearly thirty years ago, a promise I would have kept and defended until my last breath. It is no more."

He signed his name to the paper and crushed it into a second ball and placed it beside their vows and carried the boat to the edge of the pond. He knelt, ignited a match with his thumbnail, and touched the flame to the candle wick. He placed the boat in the water and gave it a push.

It floated and turned in an acquiescent circle. The flame flickered and bent in the breeze and made contact with the paper. He watched the white wads blacken within a brightening yellow bloom. As the vessel drifted toward the outflowing stream at the eastern bank, he saw the flame die and a gasp of smoke rise. He stared for a while across the water's calm reflection, wondering where the ashes would come to rest.

"I hope that finishes it," he said. He walked the path back to his bungalow with sunset peeking beneath the clouds, dressed for supper, and packed his panniers.

Twenty Five

Renati's leisurely pace proved to be short days at high speed. Chocón, Río Dulce, Morales, Los Amates, Mayuelas, Río Hondo, Teculatán, San Cristobal Acasguastlan – all were behind him so quickly they seemed as indistinguishable from one another as small print on an unfamiliar map. Guatemala CA-9 was often too rough, too narrow, and too crowded, but he enjoyed every kilometer of it. Rocinante was a champion, an unfaltering extension of limbs, muscles, and will, the purest exemplification of form following function in a machine.

On a climb west of Teculatán he was caught up by a rider on a hard-used Trek. He had been aware of the cyclist's approach and slowed a bit so he would pass. The rider slowed, also, and struck up a conversation.

His name was Carlos. He had lived in Nashville for two years while working as a technician in a music studio. He was happy to return to his family's small farm in Usumatlan, but within a couple of months he missed what he had enjoyed most about America: getting paid to work with music. He had been unable to renew his passport, although he didn't know why, and had taken to racing the bicycle he bought secondhand in Tennessee. His once-red jersey was a sun-bleached pink; his shoes – black Vittorios with red and blue stripes over a white V – were gouged and scuffed but recently polished. He wore no gloves and habitually wiped damp palms on a damp jersey. He looked to be in his early thirties and was sugar-cane skinny except for his calves, which reminded Renati of Popeye's forearms.

After riding side by side for a while, Carlos took the lead. Renati maintained a two-meter gap until they reached the crest of the hill, where Carlos accelerated away. The potholed pavement was checkerboarded with contrasting shadows and glaring sun, but the younger rider seemed to know when to veer so Renati followed twenty meters behind until his self-imposed speed limit was exceeded. He caught Carlos a third of the way up the next hill and let him set the pace. On a level stretch a few hundred meters past a village on the Río Motagua, Carlos crossed to the left and braked in front of a bus-stop bench. Renati followed and braked beside him.

"I go back here," said Carlos. He pulled his water bottle from its down-tube cage, shook it, and frowned.

Renati held out a full bottle. "Just pour it in," he said, bending to unzip his right-front pannier. He slid his hand to the bottom of the bag and came up with his spare gloves. When Carlos returned the empty bottle Renati pressed the gloves into his hand.

"For your next race," he said.

He gave his right pedal, still clipped to his shoe, a standing half stroke and coasted diagonally across the road. The sky ahead showcased a wall of charcoal clouds. He glanced back over his shoulder and saw wide-open eyes and a pleased smile.

"Good luck, Carlos!" he hollered. "Be careful in the storm!"

He met it head-on to Albinoni's *Adagio for Strings and Organ in G Minor*, which he had first heard in Peter Weir's *Gallipoli*, which he had seen in the theater seven times.

CHEF EDDIE, the manager of Hotel Camino Largo, joined him for breakfast. They had almost finished when he poured Renati a fourth cup of coffee and, with concern in his voice, asked "Do you know that it's a big uphill from here to Guatemala?"

"Yes," Renati replied. "I'm looking forward to it."

The man raised his eyebrows. "I've seen many trucks heat over on that hill. I once was living in Guatemala, but I like it better here with the good air."

Renati smiled. He could only assume that the man no longer noticed the pervasive stench of burning garbage.

"But at least," his companion said, "it's downhill to Antigua.

You are leave tomorrow?"

"Today." Renati checked his watch. "In forty minutes."

"But you ate so much!" The man pointed at the plates pushed to the edge of their table. "Waffle, *huevos*, bacon, juices, coffee."

"And, before you came, tortillas with *chorizo*."

Renati rose and extended his hand. The man clasped it between both of his, then stood and embraced him. When he drew back his expression was solemn.

"What's wrong?" Renati asked.

"*Ve con dios, amigo mío*," the man replied, slowly shaking his head. "*Creo qué quiere qué estés a salvo.*"

AS CHEF EDDIE HAD AVOWED, it was *a big uphill* to Guatemala City. Periodic downgrades provided welcome reprieve, but the scalding ninety kilometers felt mostly like the squiggly-line ascent Renati's large-scale map suggested. During a stop west of Sanarate on a knoll overlooking the craggy Central Highlands skyline, he recalled checking his pulse three quarters of the way up Loveland Pass in Colorado. It had been forty-eight at rest in Dillon and one forty-four at Arapahoe Basin.

It had also been fifty-six degrees cooler and ten thousand feet higher. And, he figured while doing the math, he had been thirty-two years younger.

Twenty kilometers back the road surface had transitioned from coarse asphalt to broad concrete tiles. The concrete was uncomfortably sun-reflective and the expansion joints were annoying but, he admitted gratefully, there was at least leeway for a truck, a car, and a bicycle to pass simultaneously. He had twice been run aground in weeds and soft gravel where the asphalt was scarcely wide enough for two full-size cars.

Around noon, while he was crossing a four-lane bridge over a swift stream in a hill-embroidered valley, the driver of an empty eighteen-wheel flatbed reached through his open window and offered an enthusiastic thumbs up. Renati waved. A kilometer higher he was passed by a 1960s GMC cabover pulling a sorry-looking reefer: the occupant of the passenger seat extended both arms out the window in an exaggerated gesture of applause. Again Renati waved. A few minutes later a Guatex truck overtook him and played a stanza of air-horn blasts.

Renati saluted and said, "What the hell?"

By the time he reached the top of the winding grade – which seemed to appear and reappear farther ahead with every rounded curve – he had been heralded by a dozen or more truck drivers with waves, thumbs, clapping hands, and horn toots. He couldn't help bursting into laughter when he was laboriously passed by a smoke-coughing stake-bed truckload of cheering farm workers theatrically mopping their brows.

Perhaps, he mused, it was unusual to see an expedition cyclist on the road to Guatemala City, which prompted him to wonder why he had crossed paths with only one other such voyager – a solar-energy designer from Oregon riding west through Texas along Adventure Cycling's Southern Tier. Perhaps, he surmised, because it had been winter in the States and summer in Central America, the opposite of a sensible plan.

On a cooling descent after a level expanse crowded with idling parked trucks, he spied the flat-capped spire of a volcano over the tops of roadside trees. He braked, hoping to view the exotic vista through binoculars, but came to a stop a few meters after the peak disappeared behind foliage.

"Did you see that?" he asked Rocinante.

IT WOULD HAVE BEEN A LONG DAY even if he hadn't gotten lost for almost two hours in Guatemala City. He arrived at the outskirts of the thirteen-million-plus metropolis a few minutes before five under threatening clouds. The divided four-lane highway was not overly crowded, but the pavement was choppy and the shoulder, when there was one, consisted of a sixteen-inch-wide gutter often occupied by pedestrians strolling in both directions. Mothers pulled children across the lanes to stand or walk on a narrow grass meridian. Chicken buses lurched from frequent stops belching oily black exhaust. A fat man in an overstretched green T-shirt yelled at Renati in Spanish from a lawn chair inside a compound bordered by steel panels propped against mortared block and chain-link fencing. Scrapped appliances, aluminum cans in barrels and bags, garbage, and a partially dismantled Toyota pickup truck spilled from between the makeshift walls toward the road. He wondered why the man was yelling at him, but didn't slow.

He passed small men in military-style uniforms – sometimes green, sometimes blue – standing with pistol-gripped stainless-steel-barreled shotguns outside storefronts. He rode straight and fast through a confusing unmarked arrangement of under- and overpasses and, luckily, exited the tangle on the correct road. Traffic became heavier by the minute; the narrow shoulder vanished. Although steel-beamed crosswalk bridges began appearing with regularity, pedestrians continued to amble into and out of the rushing flow of cars and trucks. Trees lined the meridian, now a meter across, and nonpolitical graffiti complemented razor-wire-topped walls. Massive snarls of electrical cable drooped ominously from tilting utility poles. There were *llantero* sheds every few hundred meters, sometimes two or three in a row, selling nearly bald tires.

Where CA-9 became 5A Calle his left elbow was grazed by the sheet-metal wall of a passing bobtail truck, mustard yellow with a rental-company name partially sanded off. He angled away into a bus-stop turnout and stopped to drink the last of his water. It was growing dark and he needed to watch for the street that would take him to his hotel. He would first cross a high bridge over a four-lane highway – El Puento Belice, if he remembered correctly – then a large grocery store. Two kilometers farther west he would turn left onto 10A Avenida into Zona 1.

He had plotted the remainder of the route – 1A Avenida to a street paralleling 1A Calle to 4A Avenida to 9A Calle – on the back of a receipt, but when he puzzled over an intersection unlike what he had drawn and asked a policeman for directions to Hotel Panamericano, the officer merely shrugged. He tried backtracking to 10A Avenida and found himself on a diagonal road with another policeman directing traffic around a cockeyed dented delivery van and a shorter-than-normal Volkswagen Beetle. There appeared to be some question as to where traffic was expected to detour after being waved away.

It began to rain. He strapped his flashlight to his palm and remembered that he should have been using his taillight for the past hour. He reached behind his rear rack and switched it on, wiped the gathering moisture from his handlebar-bag map sleeve, and located under the blurry transparent plastic what he hoped would be a well-known landmark close to his hotel. He walked Rocinante to the middle of the jammed intersection and asked the policeman for directions to Plaza de la Constitución. The officer seemed happy to help but spoke so fast Renati translated only "south on Twelve Avenida" and either "turn right after the park" or "don't turn right at the parking lot."

Fifty-five minutes later, doggedly astride Rocinante in traffic waiting for a green light on 9A Calle, he noticed a mustachioed doorman standing beneath an understated sign he hadn't seen the first time he rode past. He unfastened his helmet and dismounted and made his way between glittering cars over glistening asphalt.

The doorman observed his approach with curiosity, then offered a professional smile and a partial bow and, in English, welcomed Renati "to Hotel Pan American." He escorted the dripping duo down a short hallway and through the corner of a busy dining room toward a carved-wood check-in counter. Grime-streaked in skin-tight shorts, a clinging fluorescent jersey, and shoes that tapped like a metronome on the black-and-yellowish checkered tile, Renati was vaguely aware of turning heads and raised eyebrows as he led his rig through the hotel's interior.

Twenty Six

Maps covered one of the two twin beds in his third-floor room, open and overlapping: Guatemala, Honduras, Costa Rica, El Salvador, Nicaragua, and Panama. Colombia and Ecuador were with his books in Arizona. He recalled his initial travel plan – crossing from Panama into Colombia by way of the Darian Gap, revised after reading Ian Hibbel's account of the effort – and shook his head.

He sipped the cappuccino he had brought to his room after supper, and shifted his attention to the coming forty-eight hours.

In the morning he would take a taxi to the government office he hoped would stamp his unstamped passport, then walk back to the hotel by way of a downtown shopping avenue. He would write in his journal, choose music for the sinuous climb to San Lucas Sacatepéquez and the descent into Antigua, dine, inspect his bicycle, pack his panniers, and retire with an audiobook by nine. He would depart Guatemala City after an unhurried breakfast and be across El Puente del Incienso by ten and above Mixco a half hour later – if he didn't get lost and if the Día de la Asunción festivities didn't jam the roads, a possibility mentioned to him by the hotel concierge.

"To the day after tomorrow," he said, lifting the wide-brimmed white-porcelain cup from its saucer toward Rocinante. "May it be our finest yet."

Twenty Seven

Riding out of Guatemala City was like speed-reading random sentences from random books and magazines, or ingesting spoonfuls of a stew made from every ingredient in the kitchen. So hectic and haphazard was the human activity surrounding Renati he wondered if it would be possible to live sanely in such a place while fully focused on it.

He was not, he realized with wry amusement, riding a bicycle over a paved travel route, but navigating through chaos somehow more chaotic leaving the city than entering it. There were the usual developed-world urban challenges – bad drivers, clamorous noise, signage of use only to those who already knew where they were, road hazards particular to bicyclists – but the streets seemed to have been designed and constructed by a disparate assortment of engineers and contractors and, he guessed, their kin.

Lane width varied as arbitrarily as the appearance and disappearance of road shoulder. Sidewalks displayed gaping holes over exposed plumbing. Pedestrians wandered through traffic as if in a parking lot, and parking lots overflowed into the street. An old man on crutches, unable to ford the last of the five lanes between where he had started and where he wanted to be, stood on one leg between columns of cars and raised his crutches into the air and waited.

He was still waiting when Renati glanced back two hundred meters later.

A pair of young men in business apparel rolled a grimy beige Toyota Corona backward from the bottom of a steep driveway, one walking beside the car with his right arm through the window, the other taking short backward steps with both hands on the trunk. Traffic behind the Toyota forced its way into the lanes to the left, sometimes between cars, sometimes beside them. It took Renati a moment to realize that the vehicle was gaining speed and headed for him.

He dismounted and lifted his bicycle over a curb and pushed it across cracked pavement in front of a ramshackle *llantero* shop as the Toyota rolled past. He watched until the car veered into a gravel turnout under a billboard that read in hand-painted letters: DISPONABLE. A grease-smeared boy wearing greasy blue coveralls several sizes too large was standing beside him when he turned to remount. The boy started to speak but shrugged one shoulder and sauntered back to the shop and sat on a stack of tires beside an older boy about the right size for the coveralls.

Sometimes there was a meter or more between Renati and a retaining wall, garage door, or fence; sometimes only a few centimeters. Where a machine-excavated hillside was not retained, encroaching solidified mud flows jarred his palms. An old woman sat on an inverted five-gallon bucket in the shade of a small tree on the meridian by a left-turn lane. In front of her stood two more buckets filled with bunches of red, yellow, and white flowers. It was almost impossible to see her in the tree's shadow, but she seemed content to stare into the oncoming traffic.

He passed a low stick-and-plywood building selling melons and bananas beside a sports-car dealership guarded by a palisade of prison-quality steel bars. Across the entrance sagged an extraordinary agglomeration of electrical wiring. He felt a sudden need to ride faster.

The outskirts of Guatemala City, he decided, were the perceptual equivalent of a word salad. He laughed, imagining blinders on Rocinante, on himself. Plus a respirator. The concierge had been right about the holiday. Traffic exiting the city resembled a mass exodus, as if some disaster necessitated evacuation.

"As if anybody in his right mind would wait for a disaster," he said to the chaos.

HE *HAD* GOTTEN LOST, or had at least passed the correct exit a few minutes after crossing El Puente del Incienso. The Pan American's morning-shift concierge had recommended *not* turning at the sign for Mixco, but staying on Anillo Periferico until he saw the sign for Antigua. When, after four kilometers, the road angled south and the only reference to Antigua was on a restaurant billboard, he decided to return to the Mixco exit. He doubted he could safely carry his cumbersome rig up and down the pedestrian-overpass stairs, so he waited five minutes for a lapse in traffic to dash to the meridian, and another fifteen on the meridian before braving the northeast-bound lanes.

The sight from The Bridge of Incense had astounded him. Cut into the impossibly precipitous wooded west bank of the far-below river were shelves on which clung, like barnacles to the hull of a boat, crammed clusters of concrete houses. Most were white, although a barrio sited high on the slope sported sienna, azure, and mustard. Through binoculars he observed crimson-faced satellite dishes tilted in unison toward the sun, concrete blocks anchoring a patchwork of steel roof panels, rebar jutting like whiskers, whimsically lopsided doors, bare rectangular wall openings sufficing as windows, laundry drying over sagging ropes and horizontal pipes, a fancifully irregular sixty-meters-long staircase, garden plots on nigh-untraversable topography, and, haphazardly stringing together the impromptu montage within a profusion of greenery, utility poles.

Hand-snipped from the chain-link safety fence a meter behind where he had leaned Rocinante, like a portal to five or six seconds of weightlessness, was a breach the size of a man.

ABOVE MIXCO, where profuse vegetation took the place of frantic humanity, traffic crawled up the grade like a train. It was not unusually hot but the humidity, he would later learn, was ninety-four percent. Every few hundred meters he passed a car in a turnout with steam rising from under a raised hood. Plastic jugs of water appeared from trunks and back seats as if invited to the outing.

Mandy Patinkin, Diana Krall, Leonard Cohen, Sting, and Gino Vannelli partnered him up the twisting grade. Sometimes he passed cars, sometimes he was passed by cars. For a while he rode alongside a van with its sliding side door open and three grinning Guatemalan children animatedly discussing their temporary travel companion. When an open-sided bottled-water truck seemed unable to either pull ahead or fall behind, he grabbed a waist-high metal ring behind the rear axle and hitched a ride for thirty seconds. He passed a gleaming silver-and-blue chicken bus just in time to avoid being choked by the chugging behemoth's inky plume of downshift smoke. When the bus lumbered ahead a kilometer later, two giggling girls blew kisses at him through an open window.

All the way to San Lucas Sacatepéquez he pushed as hard as he could. He upshifted and stood for the duration of "Free Man in Paris" and "Brother to Brother." He stopped only once when he remembered that he had a chocolate bar in his handlebar bag. He coasted to a standstill to the trailing symphonic chords of Krall's "Love Letters," unwrapped and ate his treat standing in a concrete ditch beneath overhanging branches, followed it with a full bottle of warm water, and resumed the climb before the conclusion of "Departure Bay."

By the time he reached the level straightaway bisecting San Lucas Sacatepéquez his legs were aflame, his lungs were seared, and his balance was unsteady. He wondered again why in such moments he craved chocolate milk. He sped past a couple of American fast-food joints and La Casa del Waffle and swerved into a Texaco Food Mart parking lot. With Rocinante propped against the building's aluminum-panel exterior he stood in the store's cold air scanning the shelves of a refrigerated beverage display. In the reflection of the glass he saw a woman and a child standing slightly to the right behind him.

"You are so strong," he heard the woman say quietly. He turned. "We've been watching you all the way from the bottom," she continued in almost-unaccented English, "my daughter and I."

The child was a miniature version of her mother: fair-skinned, svelte, black-haired. Both had triangular faces and lively bright eyes.

"*Hola*," the girl said. She reached for her mother's hand and moved slightly behind the woman's roses-on-black skirt.

"*Hola*," Renati replied. He didn't know what else to say. The woman looked into his eyes for a moment and tilted her head slightly.

"So strong," she said again. She smiled at him and turned and walked with her daughter down an aisle and through the double glass doors into the parking lot.

THE DESCENT INTO ANTIGUA began gradually just south of San Lucas Sacatepéquez, but where RN-10 divided and the thirty-seven-hundred-meter-high Volcán de Agua came into view, the grade steepened rapidly. When his hands cramped from braking he stopped above a deeply furrowed *rampa de emergencia* in front of a pink-and-blue-painted wall of corrugated metal. There were residences behind the wall, set disconcertingly close to the highway, accessed by an assortment of concrete slabs spanning a narrow culvert. Behind the houses, like rolling green waves above the roof lines, lush hills rose into a nearly cloudless sky.

His rims were hot to the touch. He waited for the pastoral calm after the first *fortissimo* in Mahler's Adagietto, then switched off his music and walked Rocinante downhill to a grassy shaded spot on the left side of the two-lane road where the runaway-truck ramp began. He tugged a water bottle from its cage and was about to lean against the vertical bare-earth bank but, touching it first with his hand and finding it sticky with moisture, began pacing instead.

He had so much energy! He almost wished it was uphill to Antigua. He envisioned pushing, pulling, dragging, and carrying Rocinante through the Darien Gap into Colombia. He laughed.

"I would never do that to you," he promised his bicycle.

He knew he should eat something, but nothing in his pantry bag appealed. He balanced his helmet on his saddle and draped his gloves over his aerobar bridge, took his compass from the left outside pocket of his handlebar bag, and walked up the middle of the crushed-stone grade. When he had a view across the highway through a row of young pines bordering the ramp, he stopped.

North by northwest, he thought.

He hung his sunglasses from the unzipped collar of his jersey and opened his compass. He adjusted it a degree for declination, raised it to eye level, and aligned it with a gap between two hills.

"Galveston," he said. "Maybe . . . a thousand miles."

He closed his eyes and pictured the map, then opened them and pivoted a few degrees left.

"A cabin in Montana, twenty-five hundred. Tok, Alaska . . . no idea. About two thousand more."

He faced north. "The Arkansas Ozarks . . . fifteen hundred. Gatlinburg," he said, turning slightly, ". . . the same."

He aimed his compass downslope to the right of the most prominent hilltop. He exhaled slowly.

"Bedford, Manchester, Webster, Concord," he whispered. "Pat's Peak, The Balsams. Mom and Dad, Gram, Boopa. Number Five Rumford Street. Twenty-four, thirty, fifty years."

He cast a glance at Rocinante resting safely in the shade, walked to a mound of crushed stone a few meters farther up the ramp, and sat. He pulled the spout of his bottle open with his teeth, upended it, drank half, sealed the spout with his thumb, and rotated the base of the container into the loose stone until it stood upright. He closed his compass and wrapped the lanyard around it and dropped it into his jersey's rear pocket, then folded his arms over drawn-up knees.

He closed his eyes and saw another map, a similar charting of roads and crossroads, place names and distances, alternatives and detours – a map of his life. He had, for most of adulthood, found it difficult to recollect all but the most significant experiences of youth, as if the years between birth and leaving home were merely formative and the achievement of independence marked, like the cutting of a second umbilical cord, where *he* began. Since embarking on his ride, however, he found that he could summon lesser details with little effort. What that implied he did not know, but he valued an emerging awareness that who he had been as a boy followed a conspicuous and constant line to who he had become as a man.

Was it strange, he wondered, that a map fantastically crisscrossed with traveled routes represented, in reality, a path between two points? Was the ability to stay true to a chosen course, despite every variety of obstacle, the virtue he held it to be?

He knew that his ride had so far been a portrait of his life. That its headwinds and climbs, tailwinds and descents, sunshine and storms, distances, junctions, and detours had provided no less a chance to revisit the odyssey behind him as an opportunity to chart the one that lay ahead.

And he understood that his self-powered two-wheeled journey of necessity was making his future possible. He had thought of it as a purging above Barrett Junction while of played-out legs he demanded over and over, *one more tenth of a mile* – as an acceptance in Texas while finishing a windswept day with the setting February sun on his back – as a cleansing in the sauna of the Yucatan – as an affirmation in the breeze of his descent into San Ignacio – as a deliverance when departing a jungle *finca* south of Poptún – as a resurrection now in the Mayan Highlands.

He was so far from where *home* had been conscientiously defined for so many years, and he was where he needed to be.

He felt the heat on his shoulders and neck and was glad for it. Perhaps he would someday recover the warm core that had sustained him through thirty or more winters working outdoors; perhaps he would never again need it. He opened his eyes and stood on the mound and stretched and turned to face the sun.

He had known how it would feel, these last days of closing on his hundred-meter target. He knew what lay behind him, what he valued and would miss, what he had pushed through and been made stronger by. He was slightly less certain of what lay ahead, but confident in his knowledge, momentum, and commitment. In one respect he felt as scorched on the inside as his sun-baked limbs proclaimed on the outside. In another, he felt as fresh and vital as he always did when his eyes and mind were fixed on a new horizon.

A *horizon*, he acknowledged while savoring the word, at the extremity of reclamation.

He tipped his water bottle skyward between his lips and squeezed and drank until it sprayed air. He donned his sunglasses, took an elongated falling step into the nearest furrow, and strode down the ramp to where Rocinante was waiting. He would mount and cross the road to Mahler's *morendo* and plunge into Antigua to Vannelli's "Wayward Lover" and Piazzolla's "Oblivion." And he would, just for this descent, make an exception to his speed-limit rule.

He slowed suddenly and inclined his head and stared over the rim of his sunglasses. His gloves, hung as they were from his aerobars and spotlighted by a flickering tree-filtered sunbeam, resembled a tousled equine forelock. His brake levers glimmered like pointy ears. The horizontal silver stripe across his handlebar bag, distended by the front pocket's contents, curved upward at the ends.

"Well," he exclaimed, recommencing his stride and smiling back at his bicycle, "I'm glad you're happy!"

Along the Way

San Ignacio . . . Antigua

Twenty Two

San Ignacio Cemetery

An unnamed path-accessed Mayan ruin rising above farmland southwest of San Ignacio, northeast of the Western Highway

The Mopan River

Guatemala ahead

A family finca west of Melchor de Mencos

Climbing above Arroyo Sal Si Puedes

Pavement and sun vanished together, one unexpectedly

Laguna Salpetén

Six kilometers to El Remate

… Twenty Three

In-room laundry service

Thirteen-century-old architecture

Templo IV

A partial excavation

Cutting stone for restorative work

Stairway to Templo IV

Once a Mayan kingdom

Tacky but genuine

Twenty Four

Maize everywhere it can be tended

Between El Chal and Poptún

A limited margin

Enfoque mágico

Home at Finca Ixobel

Rocinante gets his own bed

Reading at sunset in an outdoor dining room (H.M. photo)

A silent nightly visitor on the bathroom wall

The pond

Goodbye to a promise

Twenty Five

Decreasing speed for tumulos in Modesto Méndez

Looking back over the Río Chocón Machacas, nine hundred meters from the southwestern corner of Belize

A foliage tunnel on CA-13

Vendors on the bridge over the Río Dulce

Limóns

Limonada

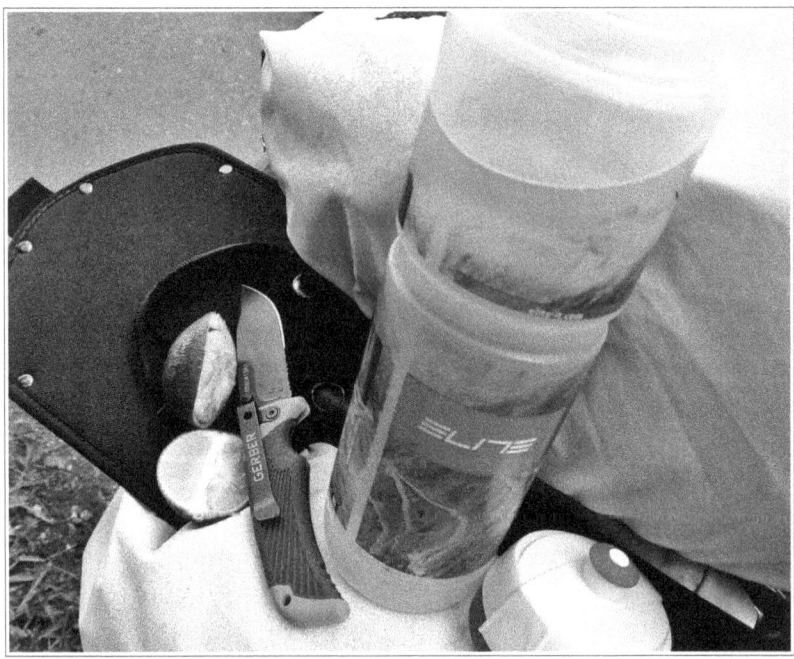

Guatemala CA-9

In response to cramped housing: the Guatemalan Love Garage

Río Motagua

One argument for a rear-view mirror

8:37 a.m. across Guatemala's Central Highlands

Climbing in good company

What goes up . . .

Around the next bend, over the next hill

//Twenty Six

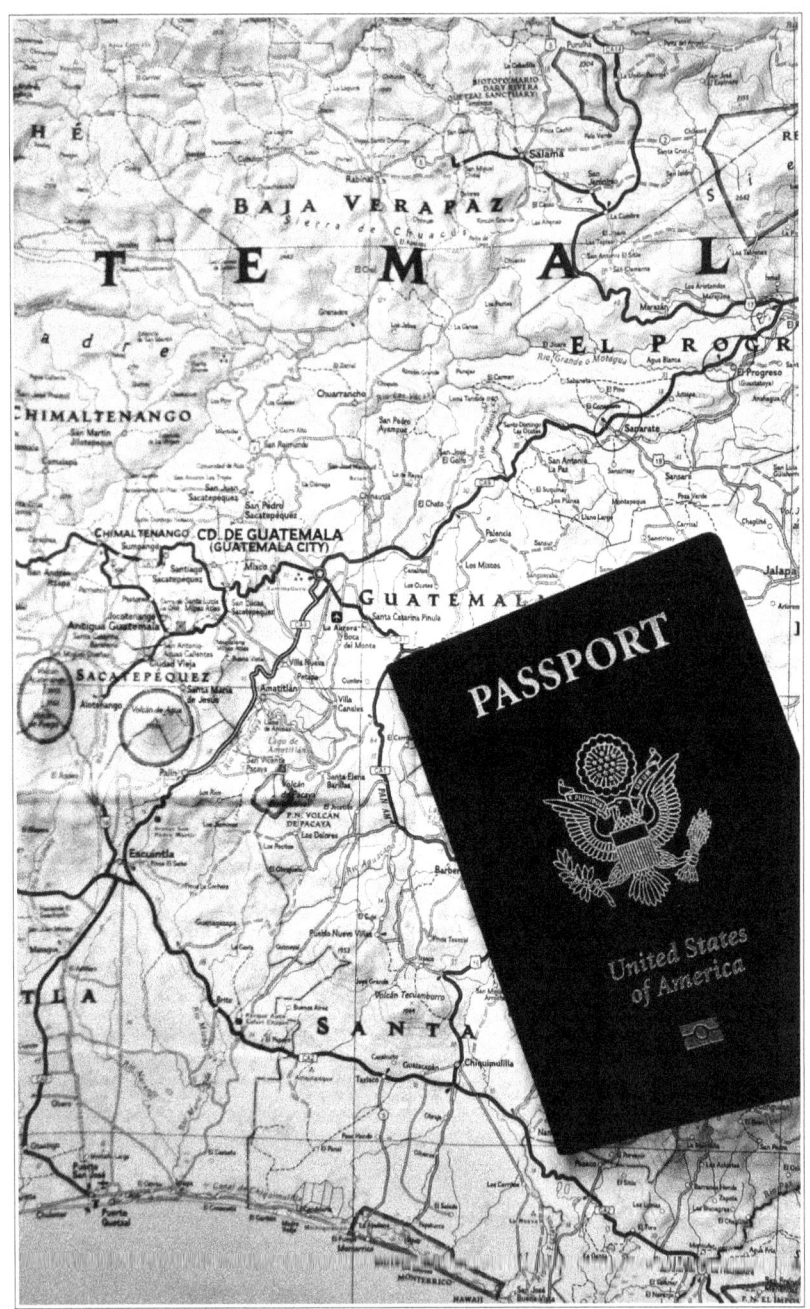

Contemplating the day after tomorrow

Twenty Seven

Can't get there from here: a wrong turn in Guatemala City

Chicken-bus service to Antigua

Wired

Pausing for the view from Puente el Incienso

. . . and to admire a photogenic bicycle

Mayan farmland

Clinging to the west bank, north of the puente

An interlude above Mixco

South of San Lucas Sacatepéquez, dropping into Antigua

Runaway-bicycle ramp ahead

Walking Rocinante through cobblestoned Antigua

Volcán de Agua

Where Spanish steeds once trod

Epilogue

From a tiled *terraza* above sunset-illumined gardens I contemplate a mountain-valley road and the coastal plain beyond. Wood smoke coalesces on a descending breeze with the aroma of distant rainfall, the breathy pulse of a bandoneón, anticipation. My worldly goods, arrayed across yet another rented bed, await sorting for cooler climes. Under bougainvillea in the courtyard below, agleam from the ministrations of soft cloth and oil bottle, Rocinante stands vigil.

My shadow, my Ragnar, is ever present.

Since choosing the path of a nomad I have affirmed what I want my life to be. Whether in a familiar land or in a place not yet found I cannot say, but tomorrow it begins.

Tomorrow is my birthday.

When next I compose in the pages of this journal I will be home.

There are landmarks on this trail
Unfamiliar to my soul,
No map for the course I've taken;
No signs save those I wish to leave
To point the way or stand forsaken.

I want another bend ahead
To know what waits around it,
One more bridge or crested hill
To tell myself, "I found it."

I pause beside the trail to rest,
To check the time, confirm my goal;
To live by what such journeys teach,
Yet understand what matters most
Is how we choose to cross the reach.

NOTES FROM THE ROAD

And so, after having composed, struck
out, rejected, added to, unmade, and remade a
multitude of names out of his memory and fancy,
he decided upon calling him Rocinante, a name, to his
thinking, lofty, sonorous, and significant of his condition
as a hack before he became what he now was, the
first and foremost of all the hacks in the world.

The Ingenious Gentleman Don Quixote of La Mancha
Miguel de Cervantes Saavedra, 1605

Inventory and Specifications

Rocinante was bred to carry everything necessary for the life of a civilized nomad; no less, no more. By the time he was on his second set of shoes he was almost perfect. The equipment listed herein was selected for quality, serviceability, and value. No compensation was received in exchange for product endorsement and, although I am grateful to the manufacturers and sellers of my equipment, I am beholden to none. Where applicable, I have provided a rating score {in braces} on a numerical scale of one to ten.

Bicycle

Frame: GT triple triangle, Al 7005, 58 cm, circa late 1990s, powder coated {10}

Fork: Surly Long Haul Trucker, chromoly steel, powder coated {10}

Rims: Weinmann ZAC2000 40-hole tandem {9}; rim strips: Ritchy (press-fit) {10}

Hubs: White Industries M15, front and rear {10}; skewers: Nashbar bolt-on {9}

Spokes: Wheelsmith 14 ga., 292mm front and left-rear, 295mm right-rear {10}

Tires: Schwalbe Marathon Supreme 37-622 {10}; tubes: Schwalbe SV17 {10}

Crankset: Sram X7 GXP triple, 44-32-22, 80mm arms {10}

Bottom bracket: Hope stainless with Truvativ GXP conversion, 68mm {10}

Pedals: Shimano PD-M780 {10}

Headset: Hope 2007 cup-style with Head Doctor {10}

Handlebar stem, primary: Velo Orange Tall Stack, 100mm x -17° x 31.8mm {10}

Handlebar stem, secondary: Dimension threadless, 70mm x 125° x 31.8mm {10}

Stem spacer/separator: 10mm x 31.8 black aluminum

Handlebar: Pedalsoft CS Type 4.705, 42cm {10} with Cinelli Cork Ribbon tape {9}

Aerobar: Deda Elementi Parabolic 1 {10} with BBB connector, Fyxation end plugs

Accessory bar: Ritchey Pro Logic II, PRO end plugs

Saddle: Brooks Team Professional with Brooks rain cover {10}

Seatpost: Thomson Elite, 27.2mm x 250mm {10} with Sugino 8mm x 19mm bolt

Brakes: TRP linear pull CX8.4 with Shimano 600 Ultegra linear-pull levers {10}

Derailleur, front: Sram X.9, bottom-pull, 31.8 high-clamp, 9-speed 44-32-22 {10}

Derailleur, rear: Shimano Deore Shadow RD-M592, 9-speed {10}

Gear-shift levers: Shimano Dura-Ace SL-BS77, 9-speed bar-end {10}

Brake/derailleur cables and housing: Shimano SLR {10} and SM-SP17 {10}

Cassette: Shimano CS-HG61, 9-speed, 12-14-16-18-21-24-28-32-36 {10}

Chain: KMC X9.99 with Missing Link, 110 links {10}

Accessories

Carrier racks: Thorn MkV Lo-Loader (front) {10} and Thorn Expedition (rear) {10}

Carrier, rear supplemental: custom hinged platform/case with light mount {10}

Bottle cages: Blackburn stainless {10} and Tallac stainless double (prototype) {9}

Bottles: Elite Maxi Corsa Scalatore (6) {10} and Camelbak Podium (1) {10}

Cyclometer: Topeak Panoram V16 {9}

Fenders: Gilles Berthoud 50mm {10}

Mirror: D+D Oberlauda Ultralight {10}

Pump: Lezyne Pressure Drive M {10}

Taillights: Busch & Muller 4D Toplight (rack) {10} and Trek Flare 10 (bag) {10}

Handlebar bag: Arkel Big Bar Bag with cover {9 before mod, 10 after}

Rear trunk: Arkel Tail Rider with cover {10}

Panniers, front and rear: Lone Peak P-500 with covers {8 before mod, 10 after}

Frame bag: Eleven81 seatpost/top-tube wedge {10}

Bicycle stand: Click-Stand Max with Brake-Band {10}

Brake stiffeners, front and rear: da Vinci Designs Stiffy

Security: Abus Diskus padlocks (2) with sleeved 10mm hardened-steel chains (2)

Tool Kit

Leatherman Skeletool; Park spoke wrench, 14 ga.

Assorted files (6" flat, Swiss flat/square/half-round); drill bits (5/32, 3/16)

Pedro's Demi 1/4"-drive torque wrench {10}; hex-key socket set (2-8mm)

Hex-key wrenches (2.5, 3, 4, 5, 6, 8mm); hex-key extension socket (5mm)

Six-point sockets (10 and 11mm); Brooks saddle wrench

Chain breaker; diamond-grit blade sharpener; permanent marker

Lufkin tape measure (6'); shop towels; assorted zip-ties; leather scrap

Inflatable-mattress/pillow repair kit; duct and electrical tape

Park CL-1 and PPL-1 lubricants; Krazy Glue; Brooks Proofide saddle dressing

Cold Steel compact shovel and cut-down Estwing rock hammer (aka "MICA")

Accu-Gage tire-pressure gauge {10}

Park TL-1 tire-lever set; Rema inner-tube patch kit

Spare Parts

Schwalbe Marathon Supreme tire (1) and inner tubes (2)

Origin8 bolt-on skewers, front and rear

Aztec brake and derailleur cables (2 each) with end caps (8)

Berthoud and Hondo fender-stay clamps (2 each)

Front-rack eyelet spacer; cyclometer bolt; seatpost bolt

Shimano cleat screws (3); fender screws/nuts/washers (2 sets)

Socket-head screws, stainless cap: M5x10 (4), M5x15 (4), M5x20 (2), M6x60 (2)

Socket-head screws, stainless flat: M5x10 (4); stainless washers: M5 (8), M6 (5)

Socket-head screws, stainless button: M6x15 (2)

Socket-head screws, Class 12.9 black-oxide button: M5x20 (3)

Lone Peak pannier hangers (2); Click-Stand Brake-Bands (2)

Kool Stop brake pads (2); inner-tube nuts/caps (3 each); assorted o-rings

KMC chain links (6); KMC Missing Link; leather and rubber washers (3)

DT spokes/nipples, 192mm (3), 195mm (2); CR2032 and LR44 batteries (3 each)

Clothes

Cycling

Shoes: Giro Privateer {10} with Pearl Izumi rain covers {5}

Shorts: Lycra (2)

Jerseys: short sleeve (2), long sleeve (1)

Socks: ultralight wool (2 pair) and synthetic compression (2 pair)

Gloves: Serfas Zen {9}, Giro Monaco {9}, and Swix (cold weather) {7}

Helmet: Bern Unlimited Morrison {10} with Sweathawg liner {9}

Pearl Izumi leg warmers {9}; O2 Rainwear jacket and pants {9}; Lowe Alpine wool cap {10}

Street

Shoes: dual-purpose Shimano MT71 {10}

Pants: midweight poly-cotton ripstop cargo (2), cotton cargo shorts (1)

Shirts: midweight long-sleeve sports pullover (1), lightweight long-sleeve linen (1), short-sleeve cotton Henley (1)

Socks: dual-purpose (2 pair)

Cabela's wool sweater {10}; Minus33 lightweight Merino wool underlayer {6}; 5:11 nylon windbreaker {10}; rigger-style nylon belt; sewing kit

Camping

Kelty Grand Mesa 2 tent {9} with footprint and aluminum tri-beam stakes

Big Agnes Encampment sleeping bag and inflatable mattress {10}

Pillow kit (inflatable with memory foam in a custom cotton case)

Kitchen

Four Dog Bushcooker Lt II stove {10}; Snow Peak titanium one-quart pot {10}

Snow Peak titanium coffee press {10}; Snow Peak titanium insulated mug {10}

Snow Peak titanium plate {10}; Sea to Summit plastic bowl {10}

Optimus titanium utensils {10}; Gerber jackknife {10}; U.S. Army P38 can opener

Foldable wash basin; pot scrubber; towel; gas lighter; strike-anywhere matches

Pantry

Bread or tortillas; pasta or rice; granola; apricot kernels; coffee
Canned protein (tuna, chicken, sardines, oysters); cheese
Dried fruit (apricot, apple, banana, raisins, dates); fresh fruit as available
Nuts (almonds, walnuts, sunflower); nut butter (peanut or almond); honey

Toiletries

Soap; mineral-salts deodorant; toothbrush; toothpaste; dental floss
Wahl Peanut hair clippers {10}; scissors; nail clippers; compact mirror
Merkur #34G shaving razor {10} with blades and shaving soap/brush
Synthetic-mesh washcloth; microfiber towel; toilet paper; plastic zipper bags

First Aid

Emergency handbook; lip balm; sunscreen; petroleum jelly; antibacterial cream
Assorted adhesive and muslin bandages; waterproof medical tape
Compressed cotton; cotton gauze; cotton pads; cotton swabs; eye patches
Hemostats (2); heavy-duty shears; tweezers; smelling salts; thermometer
Knee and ankle supports; compression bandages (3", 4", 5")
Tourniquet; suture set; surgical blades; ibuprofen; antidiarrheal

Miscellaneous

Canon A1200 camera and case {10}; Pedco Ultrapod mini-tripod {10}
HP Mini Netbook and case {7}; Timex T49806 analog watch {10}
Foursevens Quark Turbo flashlight {10}; Fenix HL21 headlamp {9}
iRiver T10 MP3 players (3) {10}; Sennheiser PMX 680 headphones {10}
Zoom H2 digital recorder {10}; Sony ECM-CS10 lapel microphone {10}
Minoura handlebar camera mount {10}; Sea to Summit travel wallet {9}
Goal Zero Guide 10 Plus solar charger with AA NiMI I batteries (12) {10}
Katadyn Hiker water filter {10}; Kindle Paperwhite e-reader and case {10}
Serengeti Maestrale {10} and Vedi {9} CPG sunglasses; lens cloth

Steiner 10x26 Safari Pro binoculars {9}; Silva Guide 426 compass {8}
Motorola V860 cellular phone {9}; deLorme inReach SE tracker {6}
Hohner Chromonica 270 harmonica {10}; Shoreline Marine whistle {10}
Clothbound journal; pens (2); paperback book; paracord (20'); spring clips (6)
Reading glasses; spare (folding) glasses; SD cards and case; U.S. passport

Stateside Inventory

Bicycle

Derailleur hanger; hanger bolts (2); Shimano bottom-bracket guide
Problem Solvers Deckster platform pedals
Weinmann ZAC2000 40-hole tandem rims (2)
Wheelsmith 14-gauge spokes and nipples (6 @ 192mm, 8 @ 195mm)
Wheelsmith Spoke Prep with brushes; Gilles Berthoud fender stay
Cinelli Cork Ribbon handlebar tape; Fyxation bar-end plugs (2)
Control Tech handlebar (31.8mm x 44cm); Blackburn stainless bottle cage
Headset spacers (10 @ 1-1/8" x 3mm, 1 @ 5mm); cable-end caps (20)
Wheel-building stand; Park TM-1 spoke tensiometer
Park BBT-69 bottom-bracket tool; Park FR-5G cassette-sprocket tool
Schwalbe SV17 inner tube; KMC Missing Links (4)
Abus Diskus keyed-alike locks (2) and key; aluminum brake-lever block
Aluminum seat-tube insert; bonding tape
Socket-head screws, button (5 stainless M6x15, 43 Class 12.9 oxide M5x20)
Stainless washers (80 M5, 4 M6); 6mm tap; assorted hex keys
Topeak Panoram V16 cadence transmitter/pickup

Miscellaneous

Pants (lightweight cargo); shorts (cargo); Exofficio insect scarf; assorted socks
Blaze-orange fabric; Katadyn-filter scrub pad; tooth brushes; dental floss
Zip ties; shoe bags; paracord and spring clips; MICA bolt and rubber cap
Goal Zero AAA battery insert; P38 can opener; Fenix E21 flashlight and o-rings
Leatherman screwdriver bits; CR2032 and LR44 batteries

Pillow case and memory foam; luggage scale; clothbound (blank) journals
Towels; wash cloths; scrub pad; soap; assorted nylon zipper bags
iRiver and Canon data cables; headphones; reading glasses; lens cloths
External DVD drive and cable; HP Mini Netbook power cord

Component Torque Values (Newton meters)

Aerobar to handlebar and rests: 5; axle-bolt nuts: 8 (greased)

Bar-end shifter to handlebar: 5.6; bottle cages to frame: 3.4 (thread locker)

Brakes levers to handlebar, cable anchor, and pad bolt: 7; to frame: 9

Front carrier (rack) to fork (lower, 5mm Class 12.9): 7

Front carrier to fork (upper/inner): 5

Front carrier to fork (upper/outer): 7

Rear carrier-assembly bolts: 4 (thread locker)

Rear carrier to dropouts (6mm stainless): 7 (thread locker)

Rear carrier to seat stays (5mm Class 12.9): 7 (thread locker)

Cassette sprocket to hub: 40; crankset to bottom bracket: 50

Pedals to crank arm: 35; cleats to shoe plates: 4 (spec'd 5-6 strips plate threads)

Front derailleur to cable clamp: 5; seat-tube clamp: 6

Rear-derailleur bracket spindle: 9; cable clamp: 6; guide pulley: 3.4

Fenders to fork crown: 5; to stay bolts: 2

Handlebar stem (primary) to threadless fork tube: 12

Handlebar stem (primary) to upper handlebar: 5.4

Handlebar stem (secondary) to threadless fork tube: 12

Handlebar stem (secondary) to lower handlebar: 5.4

Handlebar-bag mounts to lower handlebar: 5

Seatpost to saddle rails: 6.8; seat-tube clamp: 8

Wheel-spoke tension, front: 95 to 110 (23-24 per Park TM-1)

Wheel-spoke tension, rear, left side: 70-77 (20-21 per TM-1)

Wheel-spoke tension, rear, right side: 115-130 (24.5-25.5 per TM-1)

Saddle placement: maximum forward position at 16°; tire pressure at 85 psi

Weights (pounds)

Item	Weight	Item	Weight
Bicycle/fixed accessories	36.0	Compass	0.1
Panniers/covers (4)	9.8	Cell phone/case	0.4
Handlebar bag/cover	3.2	Emergency tracker	0.7
Pantry bag/cover	1.5	Journal	0.9
Tools/parts	4.7	Jackknife	0.3
Quick-access tools	0.6	Water filter	1.4
First-aid kit	3.0	Front lock/chain	1.9
Spare tire/tubes	1.9	Rear lock/chain	4.4
Tire-repair kit	0.8	Day pack	1.3
Toiletries kit	3.1	Camp shovel/cover	2.2
Power cords	1.2	Camp hammer	0.8
Sewing kit	0.3	Headlamp	0.3
Kitchen	1.4	Flashlight	0.3
Solar-charging kit	2.0	Click-Stand	0.2
Miscellaneous chargers	0.7	Paperback book	0.4
Tent	1.7	Wallet/passport	0.2
Rain fly	1.4	Ebook/cover	0.7
Tent stakes/footprint	2.1	Voice recorder/clamp/mic	0.3
Tent poles	1.0	HP Mini/case	3.3
Sleeping bag	3.3	MP3 players (3)	0.6
Mattress	1.8	Sunglasses/case	0.2
Pillow kit	0.7	Reading glasses/case (2)	0.2
Bicycle cover	0.6	Paracord/clips	0.3
Cycling clothes	1.7	SD cards/batteries	0.4
Cold-cycling wear	0.9	Sunscreen	0.4
Wet-cycling wear	1.9	Water, 6 @ 33 oz	13.2
Midweight pants	1.5	Water, 1 @ 21 oz	1.4
Lightweight pants	0.8	Granola	~0.8
Long-sleeve shirt	0.6	Coffee	~0.8
T-shirt	0.3	Dried fruit/nuts	~1.0
Socks (2 pair)	0.4	Fresh fruit	~1.0
Shorts	0.6	Bread/pasta/rice	~2.0
Windbreaker	0.4	Canned protein	~2.0
Wool underlayer	1.0	Nut butter/honey	~2.9
Wool sweater	1.3	Total = 135.0	
Dual-purpose shoes	2.7	Cycling clothes (worn)	1.7
Camp pants/shirt	2.3	Helmet/liner (worn)	1.2
Harmonica	0.6	Cycling shoes (worn)	1.9
Camera/tripod	0.9	Watch (worn)	0.1
Binoculars	0.7	Sunglasses (worn)	0.1

Observations and Alterations

Although I am inclined to overbuild and overplan, I have never regretted either. I am also inclined to under-tech, by which I mean, for example, given a choice between a paper map and compass or a GPS receiver, I would opt for the map and compass, learn how to proficiently read both, enjoy the task's inherent simplicity and self-reliance, and spend the savings elsewhere.

Which, to borrow from Robert B. Parker, I did.

The following pages are not a report on "the best of bicycle touring in (year)," but, solely and expressly, my experience-based observations on equipment I selected for an expedition ride of indeterminate distance and duration. Ultimately, no matter what the year, no matter what advances have been achieved in metallurgy or bearing design or coating composition or fabric technology – and, of course, regardless of fads, trends, and marketing ploys – the sensible standard for equipment selection will always be the answer to one question:

What do *you* require of *your* self-propelled two-wheeled machine?

I admire a craftsman-built lugged-steel-tubing bicycle frame, but while searching for one that satisfied my expedition requirements I chanced upon a used aluminum-framed bicycle with geometry that piqued my interest. I bought it, studied it, rode it 700 miles, then stripped and refinished and adorned the frame with components and accessories that I believed would suit my needs. Perfection, I realized midway into the build, would have required the addition of down-tube shift-lever and bottle-cage bosses. Yes, I became accustomed to bar-end controls and found their performance satisfactory, but long cable runs and vulnerability to damage make them a distant second choice to levers on the down tube: access is comfortable and easy, cable runs are short and direct with no need for housing, and levers are protected.

Regarding brake/shift-lever integration, I prefer these controls to function separately and exclusively (I have no objection to repositioning my hands while riding). Choosing between rim and drum brakes is a matter of comparing efficiency, complexity, reliability, serviceability, and cost. (I also have no objection to being mindful of rim temperature and braking-surface wear.)

My alternate frame, had one been necessary, was a Soma Saga.

To accommodate a handlebar bag that sat too high and to make room for aerobars, I installed a second stem with a cut-down bar, sizing the Surly fork's steerer tube accordingly and adding rubber bumpers for top-tube protection. Weight over the steering axis was lowered, and the partial bar provided uncluttered accessory installation and, inside, discrete weather-resistant storage.

Arkel's Big Bar Bag achieves storage separation, accessibility, and mounting ease. Like other large bags, however, it sits high. The internal frame of the bag I received was cut crooked, as if with a dull tool, and I found the single aluminum stiffener insufficient. I squared the crooked frame, drilled the original (upper) brace, and installed a second (lower) plate to improve torsional rigidity and to provide metal-to-metal attachment for mounting-hardware fasteners.

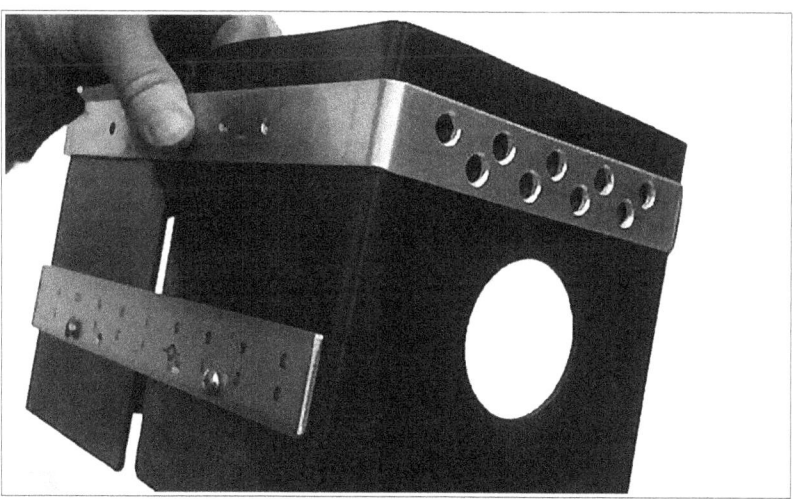

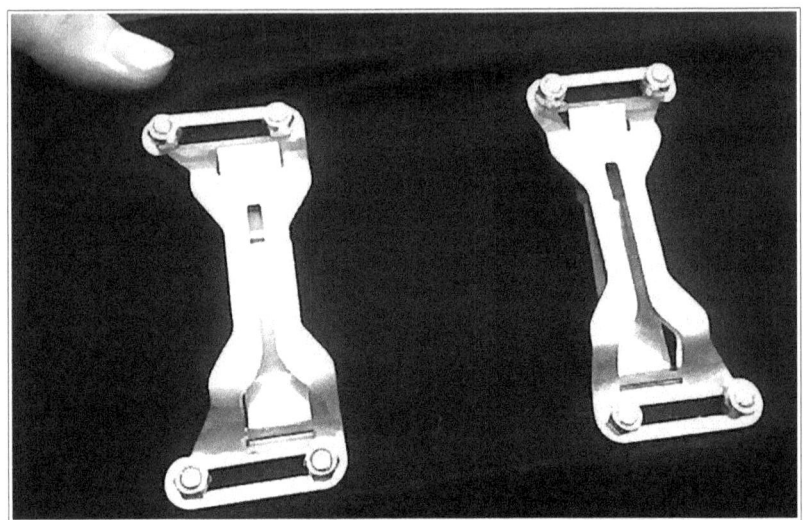

Exterior view of mounting hardware secured through to aluminum (previously to plastic) at the bottom

The resulting lowered position of the bag – as well as its fitment and accessibility under aerobars – is superior. Arkel's map case and rain cover perform exceptionally well in the conditions for which they are designed.

Interior view, sans yellow liner (a bright and helpful idea)

Aerobars were new to me, but I had in years past – uncomfortably, briefly, and without much control – rested my forearms between brake-lever hoods with my fingertips touching. When Amelia Peabody said in *Curse of the Pharaohs* that she has "no objection to comfort so long as it does not interfere with more important activities," she may have been referring to expedition bicycling. Or, perhaps she just meant electricity.

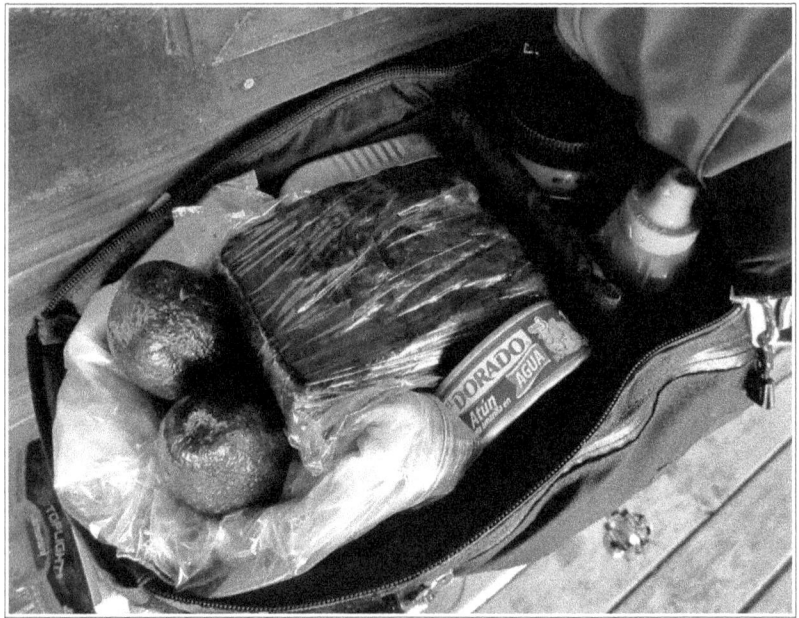

Except for upgrading from hook-and-loop to a clip/strap system for carrier attachment (or, better still, to clips that mate to a bag-specific rack), Arkel's Tailrider and its integrated cover could not be better.

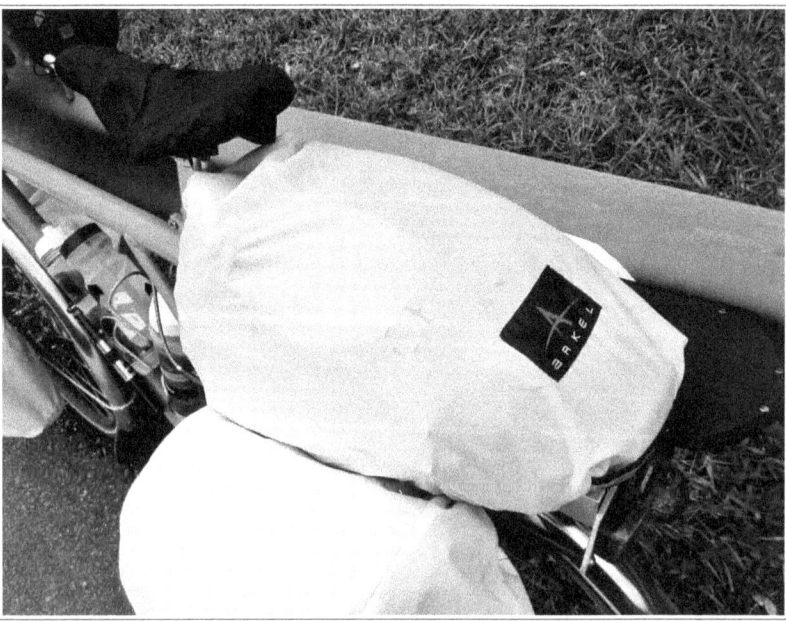

In northern Belize I dropped my Click-Stand Max folding bicycle support and backtracked nine miles in extreme heat and humidity before spotting it at the side of the road. It was worth the effort. If the rubber "Fat Foot" was molded around a steel insert, shaft push-through could be eliminated. This is one fine bicycling accessory.

Unlike Zefal's Magnum water bottle . . .

Now it has a reason to leak. Okay for storing rice and beans. One would think that, with decades of manufacturer experience, leaky water bottles would be a solved problem.

I replaced these Zefal drippers with six Elite Maxi Corsa Scalatores.

I like a saddle that requires regular care, protection from rain, and 500 to 700 miles of riding to fit perfectly. And it seems to like me.

This prototype Tallac stainless bottle cage substituted nicely for an under-tube cage mount. After silver-brazing the (formerly) loose upper-lower connection point and fitting the top cage with a 21-ounce bottle, it performed well.

I cannot imagine a better tire for long-distance (primarily paved-road) touring than Schwalbe's Marathon Supreme. Flat stretches feel like gentle downhills, and gentle uphills feel flat. It hardly seems fair.

For the same reason that I prefer a chest of drawers to a trunk for clothes organization, I like a pannier with compartments. Everything has a place, and anything can be found quickly in the dark if necessary. I prefer understated colors and fabrics that are not heavily coated, which is to say that I want visibility and rain protection to be optional, removable, and separately replaceable. Four Lone Peak P-500 bags suited my needs perfectly: each rear zippered compartment holds a liter bottle of water, and bright-yellow covers are at the ready in mesh pockets. I kept the left-rear cover installed at all times for visibility in traffic, rotating it once a month with the other three to balance sun fading.

The bags as sold, unfortunately, needed help.

Internal plastic-frame deformation indicates a likely future failure.

Carrying 17 to 20 pounds per bag, the once-flat panel becomes concave while leveraged strain at the fastener perforations causes splitting. Arguably, fastener pull-through will eventually occur (even with the thicker plastic Lone Peak uses in that area). This can be prevented either by the installation of fender washers or a panel-spanning plate.

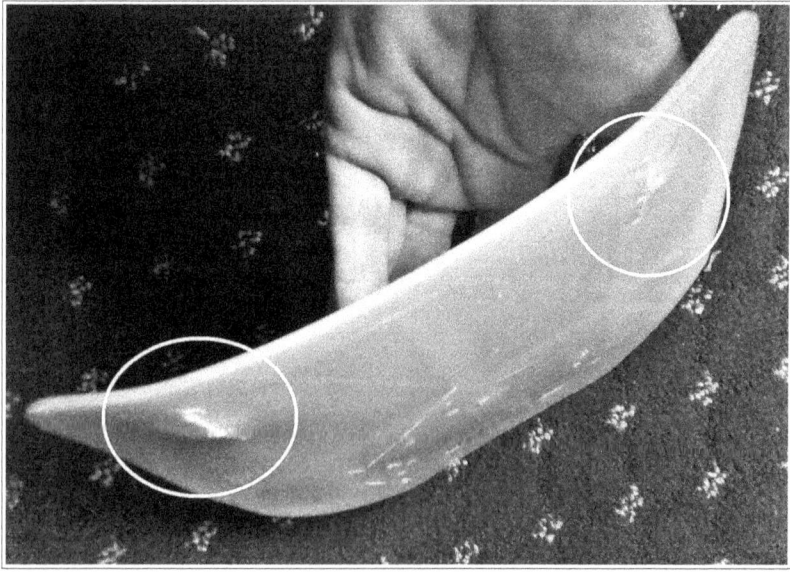

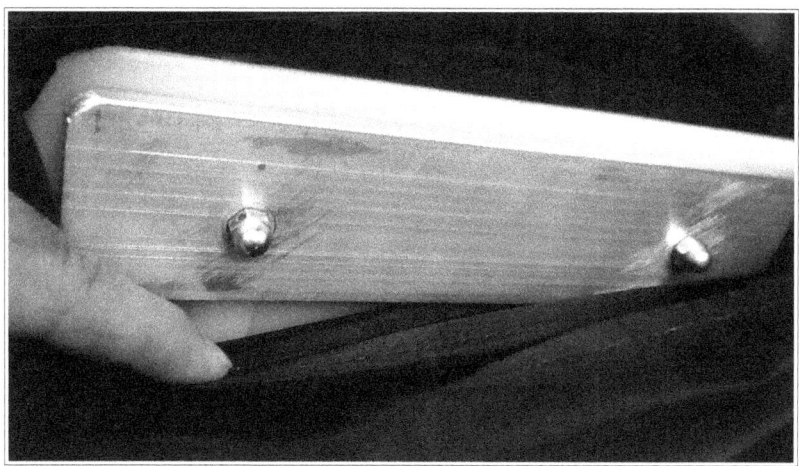

Quarter-inch-thick aluminum secured with longer screws holds the pannier squarely against the carrier and keeps bag-weight stress optimally distributed.

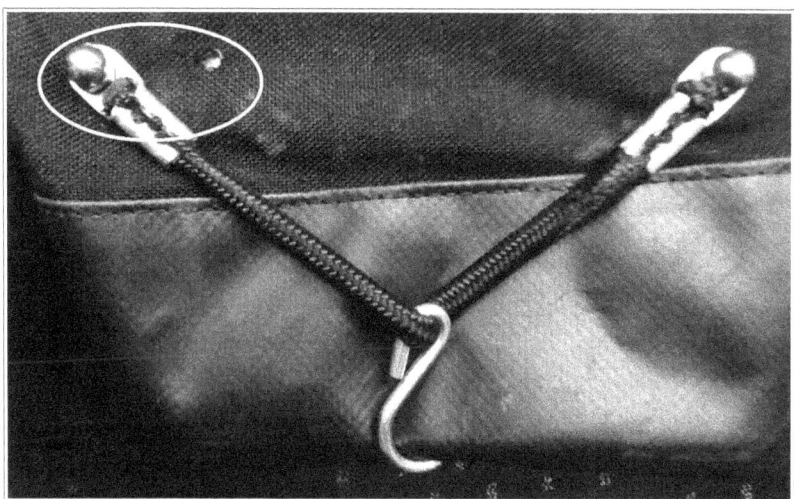

By repositioning the shock-corded lower attachment, carrier-tube damage from acorn-nut contact is eliminated.

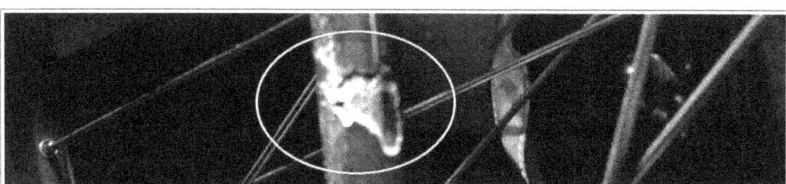

Thorn's super-strong rear carrier is attached by an M6 stainless-steel bolt after drilling and tapping the frame's original M5 hole.

Elongating the Thorn Lo-Loader's bottom mounting holes permits attachment with two bolts (M5 Class 12.9), rather than one.

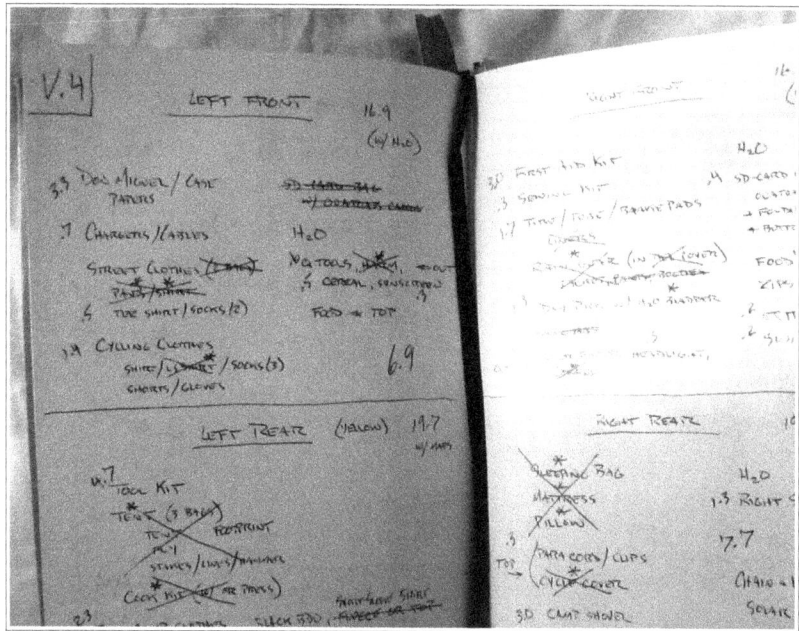

Pannier balance can only be achieved by knowing what, where, and how much. It is best to sensibly arrange one's necessaries.

Removing bags to get to bags is a nuisance, and tent poles can be problematic – they are long, they clatter, and they wear holes in fabric. I would rather unscrew a knob, tilt a platform/case forward, and lift off a pannier (while easily accessing safely stowed tent poles).

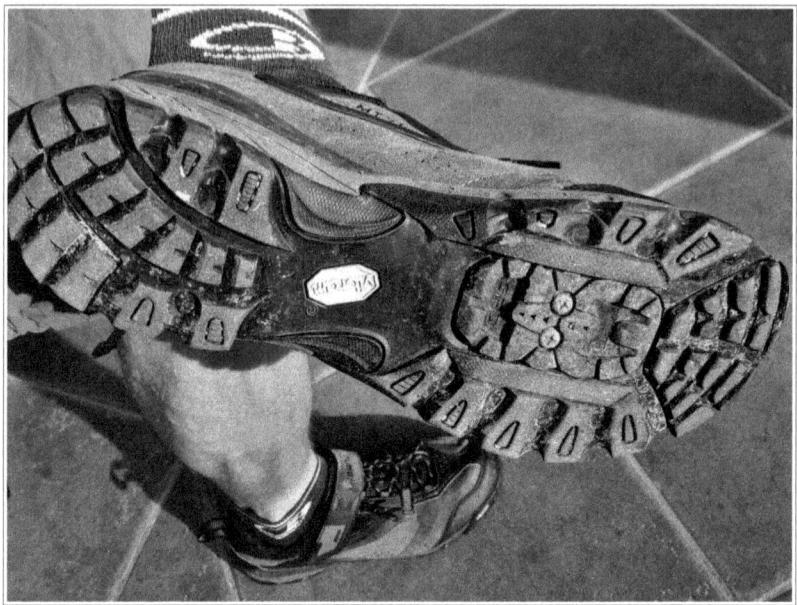

I wore my Shimano MT71 shoes only off the bicycle, but I liked having the cleat-attachment option. Better to have it and not need it than need it and . . .

These Pearl Izumi shoe covers were better than nothing until my feet became soaked, at which time *nothing* would have been better. "Waterproof" tape is a weak link when adhered to stretchy fabric. I should have known better.

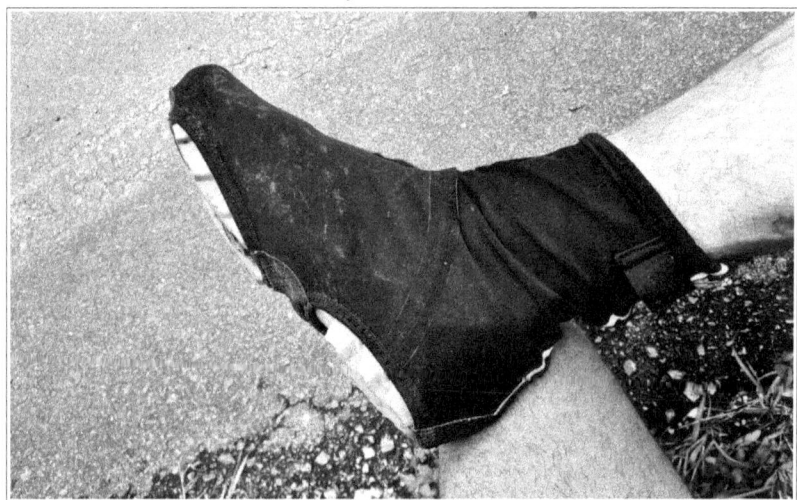

Full fenders are imperative for comfortable all-weather expedition riding. Gilles Berthoud's are exceptional – provided one takes time to make them fit perfectly and securely. In Rocinante's case, that meant some customization.

I have for years heated, and often cooked, with a wood stove. Four Dog's titanium version not only functions efficiently with a variety of tree found fuel – grass, twigs, dry cow manure, bad news – it weighs 159 pounds less than a Jøtul F602 and fits inside a one-quart pot.

Soundtrack for a Self-Propelled Ride

Albinoni, Tomaso: Adagio for Strings and Organ in G Minor (Berliner Philharmoniker)

Ambrosia: You're the Only Woman; Biggest Part of Me

America: A Horse with No Name; Tin Man; Sister Golden Hair

Animals, The: House of the Rising Sun

Art of Noise: The Seduction of Claude Debussy (album)

Benatar, Pat: Heartbreaker

Bennett, Tony: Who Can I Turn To

Blood, Sweat and Tears: You've Made Me so Very Happy

Bond: Libertango

Bonet, Maria Del Mar: La Canço de Na Ruixa Mantells

Bread: Diary; If; Guitar Man; Aubry

Brennan, Walter: Old Rivers; Conversation With a Mule; Happy Birthday Old Folk; Old Rivers' Trunk; It Takes a Heap of Living

Brooks, Garth: The River

Browne, Jackson: The Pretender

Campbell, Glen: By the Time I Get to Phoenix; Wichita Lineman; Galveston

Charlie Daniels Band, The: The Devil Went Down to Georgia

Cirque de Soleil: Allegria; Querer

Cohen, Leonard: I'm Your Man; Everybody Knows

Cole, Nat King: The Very Thought of You; Unforgettable; Mona Lisa; Too Young; Tenderly; Non Dimenticar; Funny; Wish I Were Somebody Else

Collins, Judy: The Blizzard

Colvin, Shawn: Call it a Loan

Crawford, Michael: Phantom of the Opera; All I Ask of You; The Music of the Night; Wishing You Were Somehow Here Again

Croce, Jim: Operator; Photographs and Memories; I'll Have to Say I Love You in a Song

Del Rio, Rebekah: Llorando

Denver, John: Annie's Song

Dire Straits: Sultans of Swing

Eagles: Hotel California; I Can't Tell You Why; New Kid in Town; Sad Cafe; After the Thrill is Gone

Earth, Wind & Fire: That's the Way of the World

Electric Light Orchestra: Telephone Line

Electrocutango: Felino

Evanescence: Fallen

Fogelberg, Dan: Our Last Farewell; Sutter's Mill; Longer; Leader of the Band; Make Love Stay; Same Old Lang Syne; Seeing You Again; There's a Place in the World for a Gambler; Ghosts; Nether Lands; Rhythm of the Rain; Bones in the Sky; Forefathers; Tell Me to My Face; Tucson, Arizona; Stars

Foreigner: I Want to Know What Love Is

Good, Nancy: Blue; Jenny's Dresser

Green, Lorne: An Ol' Tin Cup; Ringo

Guess Who, The: These Eyes; American Woman

Haggard, Merle: Sing Me Back Home; Silver Wings

Harris/Reitherman: The Bare Necessities

Heart: Dog & Butterfly; Nothin' at All; All I Wanna Do is Make Love to You

Henley, Don: New York Minute; The Heart of the Matter; The End of the Innocence; The Last Worthless Evening

Humperdinck, Engelbert: Release Me

Iglesias, Julio: Caruso

Joel, Billy: Piano Man; Travelin' Prayer; The Stranger

John, Elton: Candle in the Wind (1973); Your Song; Someone Saved My Life Tonight

Journey: Who's Crying Now; Send Her My Love

Juno Reactor: Navras

Kelly, Gene: Singin' in the Rain

Kern, Kevin: Embracing the Wind (album)

Kiley, Richard: The Impossible Dream

Krall, Diana: Black Crow; Love Letters; Departure Bay; I Remember You; Maybe You'll be There; I Get Along Without You Very Well; The Look of Love

Lanza, Mario: And This is My Beloved

Led Zeppelin: Stairway to Heaven

Lennox, Annie: A Whiter Shade of Pale

Lightfoot, Gordon: The Wreck of the Edmund Fitzgerald

Little River Band: Cool Change

Loggins and Messina: House at Pooh Corner

Looking Glass: Brandy

Mahler, Gustav: Ich bin der Welt abhanden gekommen; Adagietto, No. 5

Martino, Al: Mary in the Morning; Autumn Leaves

Massive Attack: Superpredators

Mathis, Johnny: Chances Are; Misty; A Certain Smile; When I am With You; Whistling in the Dark; I've Grown Accustomed to Her Face; It's Not for Me to Say; The Shadow of Your Smile; Wild is the Wind

McLachlan, Sarah: Adia; Possession; Wait; Good Enough; Circle; Ice; Hold On; Do What You Have to Do; Building a Mystery; Full of Grace; Angel

McLean, Don: Crying; Chain Lightning; It's Just the Sun; And I Love You So; Castles in the Air; Vincent (always played twice)

Meatloaf: Paradise by the Dashboard Light

Michaels, George: Father Figure; Careless Whisper; One More Try; Cowboys and Angels

Mitchell, Brian Stokes: The Impossible Dream

Mitchell, Joni: Court and Spark (album); Cactus Tree

Moody Blues: I Know You're Out There Somewhere; Question

Morricone, Enio: Once Upon a Time in the West (album)

Nelson, Willie: Pancho and Lefty; My Heroes Have Always Been Cowboys; Angel Flying Too Close to the Ground; Always on My Mind; You Don't Know Me; The Last Thing I Needed First Thing This Morning; Tougher Than Leather

Outlaws, The: Green Grass and High Tides; Ghost Riders in the Sky

Pablo Cruise: A Place In the Sun; Atlanta June; Never See That Girl Enough; Zero to Sixty in Five

Patinkin, Mandy: Experiment (album)

Piazzolla, Astor: Oblivion

Pink Floyd: Comfortably Numb; Time; Welcome to the Machine

Price, Ray: For the Good Times; Best Thing That Ever Happened to Me

Queen: Bohemian Rhapsody

Queensryche: Another Rainy Night; Silent Lucidity

Reddy, Helen: Delta Dawn

Reeves, Jim: I Fall to Pieces; Am I That Easy to Forget; Little Ole Dime; In the Misty Moonlight; I'm Gettin' Better; Am I Losing You; The Blizzard; Four Walls; He'll Have to Go

Riders in the Sky: Autumn on the Trail; The Arms of My Love

Robbins, Marty: Big Iron; El Paso; Ballad of the Alamo

Santana: Smooth

Seals and Crofts: We May Never Pass this Way Again

Seger, Bob: Turn the Page; Beautiful Loser

Sellers, Elizabeth: Out of Ashes

Snow, Hank: Old Shep; Letter Edged in Black

Steely Dan: Rikki Don't Lose That Number; Barrytown

Sting: A Thousand Years; Desert Rose

Strauss, Richard: Op. 35, Fantastic Variations on a Theme of Knightly Character (André Previn)

Styx: Suite Madame Blue

Supertramp: Crime of the Century; From Now On; School; Goodbye Stranger; The Logical Song; Even in the Quietest Moments; Give a Little Bit; Ain't Nobody But Me; Breakfast in America

Tears for Fears: Everybody Wants to Rule the World

Three Dog Night: Pieces of April

Toto: Africa; Rosanna

Vannelli, Gino: A Pauper in Paradise (album); Canto (album); Brother to Brother; Wild Horses; If I Should Lose This Love; Storm at Sunup; Father and Son; Hurts to Be in Love; Black Cars; Where Am I Going; Inconsolable Man

Williams, Andy: Red Roses for a Blue Lady; Days of Wine and Roses

Young, Neil: Harvest Moon

By Michael Russell

Honor Student

Once Upon a Time on a Bicycle

Winterdanse: The Misplaced Art of Snow Ballet

The Unfounding of America: A Countdown to Too Late

Forthcoming

Little Girl, Big Lie

Knights of the Eleventh Hour

The Inquisition of Don Miguel

Also from Nonesmanneslond

Paw to Pointe: An Irrefutable Coalition of
Canine Wisdom and Ballet Truth

by Sallyann Mulcahy

About the Author

Michael Russell had never heard of bicycle touring when, at the start of his eighth-grade summer vacation, he lashed a canvas pup tent and flannel-lined sleeping bag to his three-speed Raleigh and rode from his home in southern New Hampshire to his grandmother's farm on the Blackwater River. He was unaware at the time that others similarly journeyed and that such journeys could change, or even save, one's life. His passion for self-propelled physical endeavors led to his winning three world cups in ballet skiing and the creation of SnowDance — a first-of-its-kind theatrical dance company on skis — and inspirited a life-long dedication to achieving excellence in every quest. He has been a business manager, photographer, musician, stage actor, U.S. Freestyle Ski Team captain, teacher, bartender, logger, mechanic, motorcoach operator, builder, and un-compromising advocate for individual rights. He wrote the young-adult novel *Honor Student* in 1989 and a second edition thirty years later, *Once Upon a Time on a Bicycle* in 2018, *Winterdanse: The Misplaced Art of Snow Ballet* in 2022 (recipient of the International Skiing History Association's Ullr Award), and *The Unfounding of America: A Countdown to Too Late* in 2024. He resides off-grid in a secluded mountain valley with his wife, German shepherds, and wild-animal neighbors. He is not on social media.

www.ingramcontent.com/pod-product-compliance
Lightning Source LLC
Chambersburg PA
CBHW051543010526
44118CB00022B/2557